BY THE SAME AUTHOR
STAMP ALBUM

Coming Attractions

TERENCE STAMP

BLOOMSBURY

First published 1988
Copyright © 1988 by Terence Stamp

Bloomsbury Publishing Ltd, 2 Soho Square, London W1V 5DE

British Library Cataloguing in Publication Data
Stamp, Terence
Coming attractions.
1. Stamp, Terence   2. Actors — Great
Britain — Biography
I. Title
792′.028′0924   PN2598.S7/

ISBN 0–7475–0186–6

PICTURE CREDITS

The author and publishers are grateful to the following for permission to reproduce black and white halftones: Camera Press/photo by Tom Blau (p.195); John Cowan (nos 4, 5, 6 and p.207); *Daily Mirror* (p.63); *Kentish Gazette* (p.131); *Scotsman* (p.157). The remaining halftones are from the author's collection.

Phototypeset by Falcon Graphic Art Ltd
Wallington, Surrey
Printed in Great Britain by
Butler & Tanner Ltd, Frome and London

CONTENTS

'The stage is like a religion; you dedicate yourself to it and suddenly you find that you don't have time to see your friends, and it's hard for them to understand. You don't see anybody. You're all alone with your concentration and your imagination and that's all you have. You're an actor.'

James Byron Dean

ILLUSTRATIONS

One
Two-Year Start

'Good morning, Mrs S. I bet you feel proud today!' Mum, with her arms stretched around the dustbin, and a hastily tied turban cascading over her specs, looked up, red-faced. She hated being caught uncoiffed at any time. Daisy Straffon from next door thrust the *Daily Mail* over the fence. Smack in the middle of the front page was the headline USTINOV'S *BILLY BUDD* WILL HAVE UNKNOWN STAR'. Barry Norman, basset-hound of Fleet Street, had sniffed out the story a day in advance of my press launch. He went on to surmise that I'd signed a £75,000 contract. This must have come as a huge shock to Mum, who was under the impression that I appeared in the odd play now and then, as a hobby more than anything else. She accepted Daisy's invitation for a 'drop of short' in celebration, and the municipal Borough of West Ham's refuse disposal unit went on its way one load light that day.

The Tuesday morning ritual of who put out the dustbin had been a bone of contention between my mother and father – Ethel and Tom – for as long as I could recall. It wasn't my idea of a good start to the day to be hauled out of bed to help Mum carry the dustbin overlooked by Dad in his haste to catch the tide and the tug he drove. Lying awake, listening to the house and neighbourhood come to life around me, was one of the few luxuries I enjoyed.

Seventeen wasn't the perfect age to be in the Fifties. I found myself caught in the drift between leaving school, with a job to pass the time, and the net of National Service (the two-year stint that had to be served before grown-up life could even be contemplated). Although, when the opportunity presented itself of escaping the nest in 124 Chadwin Road, I was taken aback to discover that the idiosyncrasies of my young brothers Chris and Richard and the numerous household chores which chafed my boyhood had become gilded by familiarity. Rather than pushing me away, these tokens of discontent now bound me in an emotional web, so strong that I'm certain even my vainglorious aspirations wouldn't have severed the ties without help.

When you look back over your life, you realise that any turning taken differently could have completely changed its course. There are people who stand out clearly and certain moments when you instinctively know that if you hadn't been there, or met that person, you would never have taken a particular road. Meeting David Baxter was one of those milestones; the party in his house above Pronto Cleaners one of those junctions. Had I not gone to that gathering, had I not met David Baxter, I might never have left home. I might even have done my two years in the Army, married the right girl, and moved into the empty front room of my parents' home.

When I was young I enjoyed the kind of parties we held during and after the War at my gran's house in Barking Road, but as soon as I started going to teenage get-togethers I realised I wasn't cut out for them, and went only so that I would feel like 'one of the chaps'. These affairs followed a ritualistic pattern: the girls would arrive and congregate in the room with the gramophone, while the boys would all be in the kitchen drinking the booze they'd brought with them. When the drink was gone, or mostly gone, they would emerge and there would be a bit of dancing as a foreplay to enticing their choice of girl upstairs into one of the bedrooms. The upstairs rooms were hotly sought after and some of the boys actually went as far as carrying specially cut wooden wedges to keep the doors fastened against other impatient couples. Baxter was the first partygoer I knew who, like myself, didn't follow these general rules. In my case it was just my ineptness which forced me to the sidelines, but for him it was a matter of choice.

Both Ray Dorkin, the idol from my table-tennis days, and Ruth Welsh, the first girl I'd met with perfect legs, were at that party above Pronto Cleaners. They had arrived separately. Ray lived locally and was always game for any kind of get-together, but Ruth was only in London for the weekend, dressed to kill in high heels. (I'd only seen her in flats before.) Ray lounged in the kitchen with the boys and the booze; Ruth in the living-room with the music, within eye-distance of Ray.

I made my way to the music, practising being invisible and keeping my eyes on Ruth's spectacular legs. Pat Boone was singing 'Ain't That a Shame'. In the middle of the room was a boy dancing with a girl who had come up from Portsmouth with Ruth. The girl was considerably taller than her dancing partner. He held her right hand straight down by her side, his right arm round her waist and his head resting somewhere on her neck. Suddenly he went into a half-speed jive, the like of which I'd never seen. Everyone in the room watched to see what would happen next. The record finished and the boy moved across to put it on again. When another girl jumped up for her turn, I realised that I was watching a master-class.

Everyone else was in Sunday best but this guy had made no attempt to dress up. He wore an outsize sweater that would have fitted the *Daily Mirror*'s Garth, and a faded pair of Levi 501s with metal buttons. The jeans must have been altered because the legs were drainpiped. They were the only genuine Levi's I'd seen. He wore a pair of neutral-coloured suede boots, soft and unlined, which were also new to me. They turned out to be the Clark's desert boot, at that time available only as rejects from the factory in Glasgow. God knows where he found them. It didn't take me too long to realise he was as original as his look. He already understood that loose clothes give a slim impression.

When his demonstration was finished he changed the 78 on the turntable for a 33 and came over to chat to me. The music he played was different from the records most of us knew. That night he put on a lot of Dave Brubeck. He particularly liked the alto sax of Paul Desmond and mimed along with the solos. His conversation was peppered with references to jazz concerts. He'd been to one at the Stoll in Kingsway where Gerry Mulligan had walked on stage with his sax hanging over his shoulder, and, as the audience gasped, Mulligan glanced sideways at his horn and said, 'Big, isn't it?' Baxter was totally free from inhibitions when he related these stories; and mimicry was a natural part of his repertoire, like a dancer or a musician. As I grew to know Baxter better, I realised that he possessed qualities which made both men and women feel at home with him. Baxter and I had many late-night discussions in the coffee bars he liked so much around Villiers Street. He went to great lengths to make his point that a man was his mind, and he could develop it in any way he chose.

My friendship with him wasn't an overnight affair, mainly because he lived two bus rides from me. At the time only the well-off families in our street could afford telephones, and I was always wishing that we had one in order to short-circuit the detailed arrangements which were required before Baxter and I became familiar with each other's routines. In times of emergency, our family did use the Hobbses' telephone next door, but it wasn't thought of otherwise. The only family I knew well who had their own telephone were the Taylors, my old primary schoolfriend David and his mother Florrie. Albert Dock 1812 was their memorable number, just like the overture.

Coming home from a Saturday half-day at the ad. agency where I was employed as a designer, a billboard for the *Evening News* caught my eye: FILM STAR KILLED. I invested threepence. James Dean had died at the wheel of a Porsche Spyder on his way to the road races at Salinas, California. The idol had been momentarily invisible in his silver car on a grey road. To think that Dean – Baxter's favourite – was dead. I had yet to see any of his films. He was twenty-four.

As my friendship with Baxter strengthened, a psychological tug-of-war complicated my life. Baxter preferred to hang out in the West End. After work we often met in Soho Square, or at the Two I's coffee bar in Old Compton Street where a young man named Lionel Bart played the washboard in a skiffle group. Once, as we were leaving, Baxter asked him to 'do us a couple of collars through'. We didn't wait around for his reply.

It took me a little while to realise that Baxter was actually contemplating a move West. I always enjoyed the forays up town with Baxter, who gradually opened his treasure-trove world to me, but these trips, with him persuading me to stay later and later, often until after the last bus had departed, were invariably followed by an uneasiness which left me clinging for days like a limpet to my old mates and haunts.

I was also doing all I could to make our house in Plaistow more comfortable. I brought home a load of carpet which had been replaced at the advertising agency I was with in Hanover Street. I'd managed to get it dyed royal-blue for a cut rate, and for months we slid around the floors at 124 like eels. None of us had any idea that 'wall to wall' had to be laid professionally. We just put the pieces down haphazardly, like doing a jigsaw straight on top of the lino.

I soon understood that the ideas I had for my family and myself became more and more refined with every social stratum I was exposed to, but they were just too big to be bankrolled by my jobs in advertising, no matter how successful. It would all take too long. I knew I had to leap, somehow, into another octave. But I was too frightened to ask myself how.

When David Taylor, my friend with the enviable phone number, received his notification for the National Service medical, I knew mine could only be weeks away. (David Taylor is a Gemini; his birthday a month before mine.) Sure enough, it fell through our letter-box one morning like a bad omen. I was informed that the dreaded examination was to take place at a call-up centre in Wanstead. I was petrified. At all times of the day and night visions of being abused by a sergeant like Ernest Borgnine, as had happened to Frank Sinatra in *From Here to Eternity*, paralysed my brain. The nearer the day came, the more intense were my fantasies.

Entry into National Service came in two parts: the first hurdle was an intelligence test not unlike the ones we'd had at school. I did the best I could. The medical was held at one of those temporary-looking places that you hardly ever notice because they're camouflaged green. It was just past the George opposite the tube.

Sitting on the Central Line on my way to the medical, I cursed myself for not boning up on some obscure malady as I'd been advised to do years earlier. The stations flashed by and in no time at all I was walking through the peeling painted door.

It wasn't at all like the Devil's Island I'd imagined. We weren't all stripped naked and made to face towards a wall, but were treated in a rather civilised and courteous way. First we were taken individually in alphabetical order and allotted a desk where we were required to fill in forms on our medical history. I had no idea where they'd dreamed up all those exotic illnesses: I'd never had any of them except chicken-pox. I thought, This is no good at all; I'll be cleaning a drill square with my toothbrush before I know it. However, I noticed, at the very end of the questionnaire, a little space which said 'ANY OTHER MEDICAL PROBLEMS'. I was really grasping at straws when I remembered I'd had quite a lot of nose-bleeds at Tolgate Primary School. Mum had been forever dropping cold spoons down the back of my shirt. And then there were my feet which had given me pain when I was four-teen. I filled in the details of my treatment. I'd never seen any-body about the bleeding, so I just wrote 'months of electrical treatment at St Andrew's Hospital, Department of Physical Medicine' in the space where it said 'DESCRIPTION OF WHERE CONDITION TREATED', and my GP's name and address: Dr Brandreth, Cumberland Road.

After the form-filling we were taken round one by one to see half a dozen doctors who examined different parts of us. I kept my form with me and the doctors consulted it as they checked me over. One of them picked up on the nose-bleeds straight away.

He asked, 'How often does it bleed, old chap?'

'Oh, not much.'

He seemed concerned. 'We'd better have a look anyway. Sit yourself down there.'

I sat on the folding wooden chair provided.

He looked into my mouth first, holding my tongue down with a wooden spatula. 'Tonsillectomy, I see . . . '

'What?'

'You've had your tonsils out.'

'Oh, yer.'

'When was that?'

'Oh, during the blackout. I was about three. Septic spot, big as a pencil point.' All sorts of facts leapt into my mind. 'It didn't stop me losing my voice, though. Most summers generally, when I was at Tolgate – er – primary school.'

'I see.' He held my nostril open and peered up it with a little torch like a fountain pen. It was really snappy. 'Ah, septal perforation. Now where did you get that?'

8

'Don't know.'

'Ever done any boxing?'

'Oh yeah, at Fairbairn House Boys' Club. I wasn't any good, though.'

He made a few notes and I passed to the next doctor. The last one noticed what I'd written about my feet. He seemed interested in the treatment I'd been given. I told him how I used to fix up the electrical machine and the foot-shaped baths.

'And how long did this treatment last, Mr – er – Stamp? Must have been over rather a long period, eh?'

'Oh, not really, only about six months – yeah, about six months!'

He made a careful examination of my feet. 'Any trouble now?'

'I have a job getting shoes that are comfy,' I said. 'But when my feet are really giving me trouble I just do the heel-up toe-down therapy they showed me at the hospital!' I did a quick demonstration. 'The pain generally only lasts a couple of days!'

When I went into the signing-out room I felt sick. I saw my card on the desk of the military official. I could read the grading upside down: it was in Roman numerals – III. I was so taken aback that for a moment I wasn't sure whether I'd been accepted or not. They'd put me down as grade three.

The official was smiling up at me. 'And what kind of Serviceman are you going to be, young man?'

'Air force – I'm going to be a flyer.'

He looked down at my card. His face fell. 'Oh, I'm sorry, Mr Stamp. You're not going anywhere – you've failed the medical. Grade three, I'm afraid.'

I tried my best to look crestfallen. 'You mean I can't even volunteer?'

'No, I'm afraid not.'

He reimbursed my travel expenses.

Coming out of the centre I felt a tremendous explosion of relief. It was as if I'd accustomed myself to the idea of going to jail for two years and been reprieved at the last minute. I looked at the clock in the George on the corner. It was three-thirty. There was no point in going back to work. I thought I might take a stroll to the Wanstead Flats, but then I saw a quaint old cinema sitting cosily next to the pub, recessed from the high street. A film entitled *Mr Peekaboo* was due to start at four o'clock with Joan Greenwood in one of the lead roles. That swung me. I jumped into the café next door and celebrated my reprieve with a bacon roll and a steaming cup of cocoa. Was that movie worth the 1/9d? I'm sure my elation added to the enjoyment, but in any case a film about a guy who can walk through walls and waltz off with Miss Greenwood is serious magic-lantern gear.

I thought Mum would be delighted about my escape from military life, but her reaction was exactly the opposite. She was offended that her eldest son wasn't considered good enough to serve his country. 'Grade three! Wot's grade three about you, then?' she said, staring guiltily at my exemption card as though it was all her fault.

'Oh, I'm not sure. Something to do with my feet – all that treatment I had – and there being lots of marching, I suppose.'

I kept the details as vague as I could. I didn't want her firing off one of her famous bossy letters and demanding a recount. (As it turned out she contented herself with forcing poor old Dr Brandreth to write and ask for the details of my humiliating rejection. She didn't bring the subject up again. She probably realised I was not displeased, or perhaps Dad explained to her that the two years' Service was no picnic.)

That night I had a dream in which I awoke to find myself in an enormous bed, underneath a silver satin quilt. My head rested on a pillow of the same material. The bedhead was also covered with a mass of this silver fabric draped to fall into folds. About ten feet or so above my head was a circle which at first I took to be an embroidered crest but as I looked more closely I saw that it was the head of a horse which returned my gaze with calm, knowing eyes. As I stared, the circle grew and the horse glided into the room. It rose into the dark sky and disappeared. At the same time my body became weightless and hollow. I started to drift quite naturally into the air. I was flat on my back and, as I tilted forward to marvel at my floating body, I saw that a cord which appeared to be connected to my navel was tethering me to the bed. I could see breath pulsing through it. The higher I rose, the thinner the cord became, until it was as delicate as a single hair. Yet at no time had I any fears about the thread breaking. My world below was becoming more and more hazy, and what seemed to be endless space above was welcome and silent.

When I awoke the room was still. I could hear my brothers Chris and Richard breathing in their beds next to me. I went across to the window and looked out over our little yard into the garden that backed directly on to ours and stretched all the way to the posh house on Beckton Road. I'd grown up in the envious shadow of that big garden, with its own orchard of trees laden each year with unpicked fruit which Mum forbade us even to touch. Now I watched the early-morning mist swirling among the trees as if from a distance, rather than from the other side of a plank fence.

I turned back into the bedroom and went out on to the landing. Curling my toes over the top stair, I slid my hands, one on each side, down the banisters until my body was straight. Then, angled like a ski jumper in flight, I pushed off with my feet and, using my arms to pivot, swung myself feet first down the entire length of the staircase. I dropped neatly on to the coconut mat at the bottom, missing the wall by inches. I was impressed. It was a trick Chris and I had perfected in our gran's house at Barking Road but had never dared execute in 124 as the stairs were considerably steeper. Nobody was about. I put on the kettle to make a pot of tea, had a wash and looked around for any jobs that needed doing. Everything seemed right, in place; even the galvanised gas cooker with its oven control: a small square window showing greasy numerals. When the kettle boiled I made some tea, and poured a cup with sterilised milk, which I preferred. Inside I could feel a tension, but there was no strain: only a feeling that I could do anything.

Being a Saturday, the District Line going to work that morning wasn't crowded. Sitting in an almost empty carriage, I watched the stations rattle by – West Ham, Bromley, Bow Road. Too comfortable to move, I decided to change at Charing Cross rather than Mile End. The sun raking through the window was warm and, as the train track dipped to make its descent into the underground tunnel, I remembered running in the outside lane in a school relay.

11

The thought came into my head that I'd been given a two-year start. I had two long years taking me all the way to twenty during which I could try just about anything. It really didn't matter if I fell on my arse. I could fail miserably for the next twenty-four months, or 730 days, and I'd still be level-pegging with all my chums who'd spent their time bulling up and doing whatever you did in the Forces.

The train had just left Mile End when I asked myself what I would like to do in order to enjoy this reprieve. Where should I be going, what should I be doing, so as to be perfectly content at this minute instead of being on my way to work in some tedious design studio? Impressions came into my head of my first trips backstage at Fairbairn Theatre. I recalled the odour of grease-paint in the dressing-room and the pink glow which lit the stage when I wound the footlights on from the board in the wings.

I drew in my breath as I realised the implications of my reverie. But it was no good kidding myself. If that was what I wanted to do, if I wanted to lead a theatrical life, then I'd have to give it a go. I had two years to see. At least I would have tried. I didn't want to grow old thinking about what could have been. Two years to have a go. I might even be able to make a living at it. By the time the train arrived at Mansion House I knew what I needed to do. The only problem was how.

Two

The Emotional Range

The next time I saw Baxter, I spoke to him about wanting to be an actor. He told me he'd been thinking about it, too. We were in a restaurant in Soho called Bianchi's. It was the first proper Italian food I'd ever eaten. Until then I'd only ever had spaghetti out of a tin which I didn't like at all. Baxter had had to pressure me to have the spaghetti bolognese, but he did me a favour because the pasta I ate that evening was the most delicious taste I'd ever known. The carafe of house red he ordered, and the family atmosphere of Bianchi's, with its check tablecloths and friendly staff, put us in an expansive mood. We fantasised about our lives as strolling players and all the things we would and wouldn't do. It was late when I got off the train at Plaistow Station, and the last trolleybus had gone, but all the long way home I recounted to myself the dreams we'd talked about and wondered which, if any, would come true.

The next day I had a call at work from Baxter. He'd heard about a school of Method acting in Dean Street which ran a weekly evening class. He told me that he was going to check it out and he'd keep me informed.

I didn't hear anything more until I bumped into him at our friend Raybold's one evening some weeks later. As soon as Baxter and I were alone for a minute I quizzed him. Baxter wasn't really sure; he'd been along to the school a few times but hadn't yet decided whether or not the guy who ran it was the real thing. It was a fiver for the class, which took place on Wednesday evenings and lasted a couple of hours. There were some interesting faces and some proper actors, but Baxter had doubts about the school having the same pedigree as the one in New York which Brando and Dean had attended. None the less, he suggested I go and give it the once-over myself.

The next Wednesday I climbed the stairs of one of those

ramshackle rehearsal rooms which added to Soho's charm in the Fifties. The self-styled Lee Strasberg of London was one Jos Tregoningo, a diminutive man sporting a d'Artagnan-type moustache and beard, with a fetching young wife called Ruby who helped out or, rather, joined in. Apparently in his forties, Jos had a papery-white complexion of the kind that is normally associated with pool players.

The would-be *crème* of the English Method were a mixed bunch, including a classic John Derek type obviously looking to unleash emotional depths, and a stunning fourteen year old called Bernice, who seemed about to explode out of her jeans. She had the habit of dragging her kitbag along the floor behind her and I always had to resist the temptation to lift her, or it, off the ground. A small powerful girl with a hawk nose introduced herself as Beth. She was to be the first person I knew to subject herself to plastic surgery. There were about a dozen of us in all. They all loved James Dean, and continued to see his films over and over, speaking of him as though he were still alive. Baxter arrived, bringing a fellow with very prominent cheekbones. He had a wide mouth which kept splitting open into a George Formby grin, showing a set of startlingly white teeth, about which he claimed blacks were always complimenting him.

On this, my first evening, I learnt that the mainstay of the school curriculum consisted of something called the 'Emotional Range' which Jos explained to us.

'It is an established medical fact that the adrenal glands rule the emotions. These glands come into action before we are born and they go on working even after the heart has stopped beating; in fact until rigor mortis sets in. When we feel depressed that means the hole in the gland is a minute pin-point – that is about four in the Emotional Range. It gets smaller when we want to sleep. It is the gradual decrease in size of this hole in the adrenal glands that governs our going down the range to one. One to nine is the opening of the gland wider and wider until ten is explosion point, and adrenalin is secreted into the blood. At number ten a normal person in real life may commit murder. And after this, in real life, a person will come straight down to seven. But that is the object of practising the range, for the actor comes down gradually. At the other end of the scale, number one, every muscle is relaxed from the tip of the head to the toes.'

We were given a demonstration by Ruby, who sat on a chair in front of the class. While Jos counted sententiously from one to ten, she went from a state of absolute calm into uncontrolled hysterics. We were then instructed to go through the Emotional Range *en masse*. I was feeling more than a bit timid and very much the new boy. We all gathered chairs and placed them in a rough line across the room and I was initiated into the mysteries of Jos's emotional techniques. I must say I didn't find it too difficult, and any inhibitions I had were soon swept away by the bedlam going on around me. Afterwards, while we sat perspiring and flushed with feeling, Jos pointed out students whom he judged to be emotionally 'blocked'. This sounded so impressive that I was on the point of endowing him with a certain psychic insight, until the blocked ones were put through their paces again and most of them stayed glued to their chairs, catatonic with fright. The next exercise involved imagining being imprisoned, with a small window our only means of contact with the outside world. We were asked to recall a claustrophobic emotional memory, and to convey using just one hand how much we wanted to be free.

The class ended after about two hours and some of the students went off together to have a coffee. Baxter and I hung back, he partly with the intention of putting sand down with the lovely Bernice and partly to fill me in on who was who. It seemed that the boy with the big grin was calling himself George Martin at the time.

Baxter said, 'He's a bit over the top, but he's the only one who is a real actor. You know, he's done rep.'

'He does gush a bit,' I said.

'It's just his way; he's theatrical. But he knows the business. Stand on me.'

When Baxter and I arrived at the coffee bar in Oxford Street a heated argument was taking place between Beth and George. It was obviously a weekly custom, this coffee after class, and as I sat there listening to the debate I realised that this ritual was probably going to play a much bigger part in my theatrical education than all of Jos's 'Emotional Range'.

George, whose 'hand through the window act' had been impressive, was owning up to having summoned no real emotion at all. He had watched everybody else demonstrating a St Vitus's dance of the fingers and, when his turn came, used a little technique, hardly showing his hand at all. Beth took the attitude that the school wasn't a place to score such cheap hits; rather, it was somewhere to discover whether or not one was capable of uncovering emotions real enough to convince an audience night after night.

I didn't contribute anything to the conversation during that first evening. I was busy trying to view my classmates objectively. The John Derek type, who had bought all the cappuccinos, was certainly a hunk, but I wasn't at all sure that any of us would go the distance. Baxter was the sole exception; his flinty quality gave him a certain authority. Despite my reservations, I felt comfortable enough. I knew I didn't have the looks of accepted screen idols like Wilding and Granger, but I thought I might find a way to make a living.

The most memorable evening at the Method school occurred when the *Tonight* TV programme came to film there. All of us were sick with excitement, but desperately trying to look cool. Each was secretly convinced that a single exposure on prime-time television would be sufficient to get discovered and whipped off to Hollywood. Nobody quite believed that the camera unit would actually show, but it did. When we clattered up the stairs for our class, the crew were already there with the camera set up. We did our Emotional Ranges like there was no tomorrow. I was chosen by Jos to portray a man being tortured. I mimed my hands being tied behind my back whilst my torturer pulled the fingernails out. George whispered to me before the off, 'Do it, but keep your head up so they can see you.' Of course, I forgot. George, being a student of longer standing, was asked to portray a tree. I don't think the *Tonight* interviewer altogether understood that these Method rigours were essentially mental exercises. In the midst of being a rather wonderful tree, George was asked by the BBC presenter how he felt. That was the moment when George uttered the immortal line, 'I can feel the sap rising in me.' The show was aired the same week. Needless to say, no one received a midnight call from California.

The Method school split my life in two. It was hard to find the words to tell my family and friends back in the East End what I was getting up to in town. When I was with the Soho group I could see only too clearly the divide I was creating between myself and local chums. Yet it was some time before I tumbled to the fact that pigeon-holing my life like this was getting me nowhere.

Predictably, it was Baxter who urged me to decide on my priorities. After I had been going to evening classes for a month, he told me that he and George had decided to look for a flat up town and asked whether I wanted to be counted in. The rent for a halfway decent place would not be cheap. If we were going to look for a good address – something which George considered essential for any aspiring thespian – the more the burden of expense was shared the better.

I was rather taken aback by the speed at which things were happening but Baxter seemed unperturbed and I took heart from his apparent fearlessness. None the less, I had ambivalent feelings about George. Although he was a sweet guy, I hadn't thought about him as a flatmate. My mind turned to my old mate Lee. I kept thinking about how he'd confessed his dream of leaving Plaistow and becoming a singer with a dance band.

I said to Baxter, 'I have this mate, older than me. He's always wanted to get out of Plaistow. D'you think George will mind if I ask him as well?'

Baxter put down the bottle of Daddy's Sauce he was reading and took a sip of his tea. We were sitting in a café a few doors along from the Upton Park Odeon and had finished a late Saturday lunch of bacon and eggs. He'd acquired the habit of reading whilst eating. Proust, Gibran, sauce bottles, it didn't seem to make any difference.

'I don't see that it matters to George. We decide. He'll go along with what we want. If he's a good bloke, ask him. It's only a flat we're sharing. It's not a big deal.'

It might not have been a big deal to Baxter, but, almost without thinking, I'd given my tacit agreement to something that would completely alter the direction of my life.

I could think only of Mum and how she would take it. How could I even broach the subject? I couldn't name a single local who'd left home. True, guys got married, but that didn't usually entail leaving their folks. They just moved into a room upstairs, wife and all. If it had happened to me, I'd have been put into the empty front room with the frost bite. Not that any girl had even looked twice at me, let alone offered to take on my family.

I took up the problem with an artist at work. He was Irish and everyone called him Mac.

'Yes, it's the girlies that's the problem. Yer ole man'll probably be glad to get shot of yer.'

'What d'you think, then, Mac?'

'Well, let's see, then.'

He ruminated over his drawing board. He was drawing a cartoon in Indian ink, something he often did when not busy.

I went round beside his stool to see better. It was a drawing of an auction room. On the stand in front of the auctioneer was a big black iron pot, and a scrawny witch-like arm was thrust in the air out of the crowd of bidders.

'We'll say yer man is all right with it, then.'

'Yer man?'

'Yer dad, he'll be no trouble. It's yer mam that'll be not wanting to let go of yer.'

'Yep, that's about it.'

Mac lettered in 'WHAT AM I BID?' 'Why don't yer tell her you're thinking of going to Rhodesia to make yer fortune?'

'What?'

'Yes, to make yer fortune. In the copper mines.'

'Could I?'

'Well, to be sure you could. They pay a smart fella like yerself a king's ransom, in charge of all them coloured chappies doing the work . . . '

'No, I don't mean could I do it. Could I tell her that? What good would it do?'

'To be trying her out. You know, look at it this way: there's going to be tears whatever. It's like pulling hens' teeth, getting away from home. You get her used to be losing you for ever, so to speak, then she'll be pleased when you're only coming up West, you see.'

'It's a bit cruel, Mac. It's me *mum*!'

'I know, lad, but you love yer mum, right? It's only being cruel to be kind. She'll be as pleased as Punch when you make a success of yerself.'

I did just as Mac advised, but of course I didn't have the blarney with which he was blessed, and the ructions at home were terrible. It was Friday, our fish and chip night, and even Chris, usually so stoic, was cowed by Mum's explosion. I watched him tuck his head down into his rock salmon as though trying to get below the flak.

'Who put that stupid bloody idea into your head, then?'

'This bloke at work.'

''As he done it, then?'

'Yeah, he did it. Made a fortune.'

'Well, wot's he doing still at work, then, if he's made a fortune?'

'I don't know. He likes to draw; he's an artist.'

'Sounds like a bloody pavement artist to me! I don't know what sort of people you're mixing with up there. What did I do to deserve kids like this!'

She looked heavenward. Chris used the pause to duck out into the passage. We heard the street door slam behind him.

'Listen, Mum, you wanted me to work up town. To better myself, wear good clothes, meet a different class of people.' I kept my voice soft in an attempt not to get caught up in her temper.

'Fleet Street. I wanted you to work in Fleet Street. Meet nice, refined people. Journalists! Newspaper people!'

Mum had worked near Ludgate Circus in her youth. She and her friend Dora used to have Welsh rarebit for lunch in the King Lud. I think that's where she got this idea about the superior species of the print.

'I don't know what your dad's going to say!' she continued.

I shrugged my shoulders. 'He went away to sea.'

'Yes, but he didn't leave home.'

I sensed that the storm was blowing itself out. I thought I would put the radio on. It was a quarter to seven by the alarm clock on the mantelpiece. Time for *The Archers*, an everyday tale of country folk. It wasn't as good as *Dick Barton* but Mum and I often used to listen to it together.

'When are you going, then? When are you starting this cockeyed scheme?'

'I – er – don't know yet. I've got to make some enquiries,' I lied.

This was obviously the right answer. It seemed to pacify her. She sat in the armchair opposite the window and took off her spectacles. She looked worn out. I took the plates to the scullery and did the washing up. From the kitchen I heard the 'Da de da de da de da, da de da de da da' of *The Archers'* musical theme. I don't think either of us listened much to the goings-on of the country folk. It was very quiet. The Tigress had roared.

The next thing I knew, an apartment was on the cards!

Gilly was a rather tubby girl who sometimes came to the Method classes in Dean Street. She had a funny lip. I don't think it was a hare-lip because she had no speech impediment but, whatever it was, it gave an uneven set to her face. George always made a fuss of her, but then he had a gregarious nature. When I asked Baxter about her, he told me that she was a receptionist-cum-housekeeper in a building in Harley Street where there was a possibility of a flat being let. 'If you haven't already spoken to your mate, you'd better do it soon,' he warned.

As it turned out I didn't broach the subject with Lee until the basement flat in Harley Street actually became vacant.

I hadn't seen much of Lee since he had started going steady, and I'd met his girlfriend only once. I often used to walk past Lee's house on my way to the YMCA. I didn't use the club so much since I'd stopped playing ping-pong, but I occasionally looked in to view the talent. Rather than going straight along Chalk Road to reach the nearest 699 bus stop in Prince Regent's Lane, I had fallen into the habit of turning left into Egham Road and cutting up Holborn Road so that I could see whether his car was outside Number 23.

One evening I'd taken my usual route and, seeing that the car wasn't there, strolled back along Prince Regent's Lane to the bus stop. God knows how many hours I'd put in at that bus stop while waiting for the infrequent trolleys, idly listening for the telltale hum of the overhead cables. I knew the trunk of the plane tree next to the stop by heart. That evening, sensing that my departure from home could be imminent, all the things I had always taken for granted were suddenly showing themselves in a new light.

I was peering at the old tree which had shared my frequent sojourns when two things happened simultaneously: just as I heard the familiar growl of Lee's Lea-Francis taking the corner opposite the Rec., the street lights came on. I saw Lee's blond hair behind the windscreen and for a moment had the notion that his energy had been responsible for the lights coming on. His eyes were on the road and, as he drew level with the bus stop, I yelled, 'Hello sailor.'

He screeched to a halt and I strolled over to the car which was in racing trim, as usual. He'd taken the side windows off although the weather was wintry.

I said, raising an eyebrow like Vic Mature, 'Travelling alone?'

Lee grinned and, affecting a similar sibilant voice (a routine we had practised with girls who proved to be a bit of a drag), said, 'That depends.' He yanked the tonneau cover off the passenger side and I stepped over the low door and slid into the leather bucket seat.

Lee racing-changed into third and we flashed past Plaistow Grammar to climb the slope, decelerating down the hill towards the Greengate traffic lights with a throaty roar that caught the attention of everybody at the bus stop as well as in the queue waiting outside Kosky's for fish and chips. We stopped at a red light and I revelled in the unrest we were causing. A girl from Sutton Court Road walked past, trying to ignore us. I'd always lusted after her sleek figure.

Lee said, 'I love it when they can't look at you!'

'What does it mean, Lee?'

'Means they're thinking about the same dirty soapy things we are.'

I looked anew at Diana Wrigley's retreating ankles as she strolled past Comber's, the barber's where as a boy I'd sat waiting for a haircut, mystified at the small purchases being surreptitiously slid across the counter in brown paper.

'What are you up to, then?' I asked.

Lee shrugged his shoulders. He was wearing a suit and a rather formal starched collar with a tie. I assumed he was off on a date. He ran the tip of his tongue over his top lip.

'You're not on the loose?' I asked.

He nodded.

'Slipped off the leash, eh?'

'Barbara's doing her hair. Takes all evening.'

'Sure she's not got a headache?'

He grinned again, wolfishly. 'Nah. Great thing about her is she never insists but she's always ready.'

'Rare,' I said, as if I knew.

'You can say that again, sunshine. Now what's your pleasure, my son?'

The lights changed. With a screech, we cornered into the Barking Road, past the cockle and whelk stall, past the second-hand bookmart with the smell I liked, past Ambrose's the barber's where I'd had my first shave, past Denny Mincer – Distinctive Clothes, past the London Co-operative Society, past Bates for Bikes.

'Coffee or a beer while we decide what to do?' said Lee.

'Coffee.'

We squealed left into Green Street, en route to Tabu.

'I've got some news,' said Lee.

'Me too,' I replied.

The sensation I'd had at the bus stop was renewed. Every detail seemed to jump out at me during that evening which contained all the things I loved about the patch where I'd grown up. It was six-thirty when I met Lee at the bus stop and eleven-thirty when I went to bed. According to the clock five hours had passed, but in truth it was one of those occasions when time stands still, there being an endless space into which everything naturally slots.

Drinking coffee, to the accompaniment of Dean Martin's 'Memories are Made of This' played over and over again, Lee told me of an interview he'd had that day at Salter's pram shop. He'd finally decided to break with the docks. It had taken some guts. He was one of the heroes of the East India Dockside: tough, funny, glamorous, a real Jack-the-lad. I questioned him closely about his motives. Soon to be thirty, he foresaw the end of the docks as he knew them. 'It's got to end, too many people getting something for nothing. You know it's money for old rope, Tel!' His whole working life had been physical: at sea, iron fighting and the last five years loading and unloading cargo. He was in his prime, but he'd obviously begun to be self-conscious about being a labourer and I wondered whether this switch to a white-collar job had been instigated by him or by his girlfriend. He was to do a short course in salesmanship and be swiftly initiated into the perambulator chain. I had no doubts about his success with expectant mothers.

A newly built cinema, the ABC, had just opened farther down Green Street. It was showing a dubbed version of *Helen of Troy* starring Rosanna Podesta and Jacques Sernas and, more importantly, the young French siren Brigitte Bardot, whom neither of us had ever seen. We pulled the tonneau cover back over the car and strolled round the corner to see the flick. The ABC in no way compared to the other local picture palaces, but B.B. and her classic line addressed to her mistress Helen – 'Do you need me for anything?' – brought a chorus of suggestions from us and most of the other guys in the audience.

After the movie we cruised around with the top down and the heater keeping us warm. (I'd only ever driven the car once, when Lee gave me a lesson outside David Taylor's house. I'd stalled the precious machine right across the Beckton Road and had settled for having a photo taken at the wheel.) We checked out many of our old haunts, like ghosts on a beano, eventually winding up at the tea stall outside the Greengate pub. I ordered a couple of teas and Lee said he'd treat me to supper at a restaurant that had recently opened around the corner in Barking Road. The new joint was situated a few doors along from Larkins, sandwiched between Spittles the florist and the stationery shop that doubled as a post office. The floor of the café was raised a foot or so above ground level, with steps to walk up before going in. Lee sat at a table with his back to the window; I was opposite, observing the traffic and passers-by from what felt like a great height. He urged me to order exactly what I fancied, and finally we both settled for a mixed grill, even though at 3/6d it cost a shilling more than the other dishes.

'Put an egg on the steaks, darlin',' Lee told the waitress. 'Never know when it might come in handy.'

And so we toasted his new job with the sausage, liver, kidneys, chump chop and all the other bits and pieces that made up a Special Grill. I basked in the decadence of eating late at night. I was bursting to hit him with the possibility of the rooms in Harley Street, but he seemed so eager to tell me about all the things that had happened to him since last we'd talked that I hardly managed a word. Now and then I flicked a look across the road at the customers turning out of the neon-lit milk bar while he chomped on his steak. We lingered over cups of tea, thick and strong, designed to keep night owls alert, while Lee successfully taught me how to blow smoke rings with one of his Senior Service.

'How are you doing with the tiddles I steered you to?' he asked.

'Not too bright.'

'Don't tell me they're not coming across.' His jaw almost hit his plate.

'It's not that, Lee. I'm so spring-loaded I practically come before I've got me strides loose. It's embarrassing!'

'Nothing to be embarrassed about; you just have to pace yourself a bit. I used to jerk myself off before a date, until I got the knack.'

'The knack?'

'The timing!' He leaned back in his chair and gave the matter some thought. 'It does take a while to be able to let go when you want. I'll tell you something else I did before I got the hang of it. I read this article about boxers. They reckoned you could sweat everything off except women. That's why they kept 'em in training camps without company before a fight. I worked out if the boxers needed their strength for the fight, and could put their energy into their shoulders, I could do the same. I had a natter with some of the fighters at the Black Lion. One of 'em told me he'd been in training for a bout that got postponed, so he nipped back to his ole lady, but –' Lee paused dramatically – 'instead of a quick splurge it took for ever to get his rocks off. He said his cobblers were like walnuts. That's great, I thought. I started doing exercises in the evening before I scored.'

'What exercises?'

'Well, press-ups mainly, but I suppose anything would do.'

'Did it work?'

'You don't think I got these working in the dock, do ya?' He lifted his shoulders up, like Charles Atlas.

'I'll try that,' I said.

'Main thing to remember with birds is they don't care if you're a bit previous as long as it's a giggle. Too many people take the whole thing seriously, whereas I keep it light. If I happen to shoot my bolt before she gets off, I laugh. I say, "Well, that one's down to me; next one's for you." '

It was dark and late when I hopped from the car outside 124. As I was reaching for my key, Lee said, 'Hey, what about your news? Didn't you say . . . ?'

'Tell you next time.'

'OK, tomorrow . . . before I go out. I'll tell you what the guys in the dock say about me getting out.' He seemed excited, as though tonight had reminded him afresh of the good laughs we'd always had together.

As I put the long iron key into the lock, I remembered the day that Mum had given me a key of my own. My first term at Plaistow Grammar. It had been snowing all day, and my hands were so numb with cold that I couldn't turn the key in the lock.

Christmas came and went and there was still no news of the flat. I was beginning to have second thoughts.

On New Year's Eve everybody except me was intent on ending 1956 with a bang. At a loose end, I took the long bus ride to the West End, being drawn to the lights as if by a promise of incident. I wandered around until I came to Charing Cross Road, where I was attracted by a cinema advertisement. It was one of those small placards in a wooden frame which cinemas pay shopowners to fix to their walls. This particular board was under one of the windows of Cecil Gee. It boasted several current re-runs, but as it caught my eye from across the street the bottom line of print seemed to swell and fill the poster. *East of Eden* was showing at the Gala, Tottenham Court Road. I decided to see the New Year in checking out Baxter's hero. I didn't even have to change direction; I just kept walking straight across Oxford Street into that hinterland where the West End suddenly runs out of glamour. I reached the little pair of old cinemas just in time for the main feature. I recall settling down into a cherry-red mohair seat as the film unreeled and the plaintive music of Leonard Rosenman caressed me like an unseen hand. I sat through the programme twice (as was possible then). When I emerged into Tottenham Court Road it was almost 1957.

On the long ride home, sitting in the front seat on top of a 23 bus, I was oblivious to the revelry going on around me as midnight struck. What had happened in the stalls of the Gala, apart from being reduced to tears, was difficult to comprehend, and even more difficult to explain. Much had been said about James Dean but nothing could have prepared me for what I felt on seeing him that evening. It was as if the whole of my inner world – so secret, so peculiar to me – was somehow contained and reflected in the figure I had watched in the darkness. What made it even more poignant was the knowledge that he was dead. His very existence was now confined to a celluloid image.

From then on, like thousands of others, I began to search for any insight: films, scraps of films, screen tests, bit parts, books by people who knew him, articles by folks who said they had met him. I even taught myself to play a one-handed version of Rosenman's *East of Eden* theme on the piano. Now I understood all the lovelorn students at the Method school; they were learning the system because they knew Dean had.

Three

Number 64

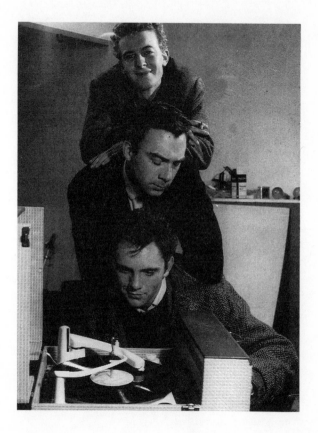

When I'd almost given up the idea of leaving home, the flat came free. Baxter phoned me at work with the good news, and I arranged to meet him that evening in a new snack bar on the corner of Margaret Street and Portland Place. Baxter seemed to know the waitress well and she gave us giant doughnuts and a cup of lemon tea each to warm us up.

Harley Street appeared wide and bright as we approached it from Cavendish Square, and extraordinarily clean compared with Chadwin Road. I kept thinking to myself, Am I really going to live here?

'I don't think we'll be able to play football down this street,' I said.

Baxter nodded his head towards the red door of Number 8. 'That's Equity. We'll be joining that one day.'

I hoped it was a good omen that we would be on the same side of the road as the Actors' Union.

Gilly opened the door of Number 64. The entrance hall had a fireplace with scented cut flowers in a vase on the mantel. I also picked up the underlying aroma of lavender furniture polish. Heavy drapes at the end of the passage prevented further investigations for the time being. An oak staircase, carpeted and held by shiny brass rods, climbed off to the right. We were ushered hastily past the open door of a waiting-room. Squeezed between the reception area and the staircase was Gilly's alcove, and hidden behind the stairs was a small door through which Gilly showed us. We followed her down the winding dungeon steps to the basement. Our apartment was at the back of the building along a musty passage. My new tan shoes from Saxone's, with half-inch welts like platforms, clattered on the flagstones. Theatrically, Gilly threw open the door, but then had to rush back upstairs to answer the telephone.

Baxter and I stood peering in, as if stepping over the threshold was much too big a commitment. We grinned sheepishly at each other and edged into the main room. Like subterranean apartments the world over, it wasn't very light, but the area outside the window had been walled with white tiles to give maximum reflection and two skylights in the ceiling prevented it from being actually dim. The space wasn't badly furnished: it had an armchair, a sofa, table, some chairs, an old, rather worn, carpet and an electric heater. One wall, in which there was a door leading to the other rooms, had a big chunk missing, as though a hole had been allowed for a window which had never been put in. In place of a window-sill was a wooden shelf about a foot wide. There was a bedroom, scullery and lavatory.

Gilly reappeared at the front door.

'The bathroom is under the stairs. We share it.'

Her tone was placatory, like an estate agent putting a gloss on an undesirable feature. She wasn't to know that in my book any bath that had a room of its own was a terrific plus.

Baxter was busy in the bedroom which housed two single beds, one against each wall. He said, 'George and I can use these. You and your mate can put beds in the big room, or just you if he doesn't want to come.'

That seemed OK to me. I had already mentally bagged the spot along the wall under the giant serving hatch for my bed which I could bring from home. We were investigating the contents of the kitchen when the phone rang. It sounded louder than before.

Gilly made for the door and paused like a pin-up with one hand on the door frame. 'Shall I get it?' she enquired.

Baxter said, 'Why not?'

'It might be for you,' she said as she disappeared into the gloomy passageway.

'We haven't got a phone?' I gasped, my voice failing me.

'Sure,' replied Baxter, trying to sound casual.

'I wonder what the exchange is,' I said.

We both rushed up the passage after Gilly who was chatting animatedly on a black pay-phone attached to the wall by the stairs. We ignored her, craning over her shoulder to see the number.

'It's LAN,' I said. 'Langham. Langham 1118.'

'Wow, that's eleven!' said Baxter, who was into numerology. 'That's slick. Eleven's a real buzz.'

'Is it good, though?' I asked.

'Oh yeah, it's a guvnor number. I don't know exactly the symbolism, but it's one of those cardinal numbers, like thirty-three and a hundred and one, that you don't add together. You know, thirteen is a four. I know ten is a rainbow, but eleven . . .'

He promised to check it out. I think it was the phone and its prestigious number that made up my mind. Not only an address in Harley Street, but a Langham phone number, to boot!

Somehow I made it back to Plaistow by bus and went looking for Lee. I recognised his rolling gait coming towards me from Prince Regent's Lane. I had long marvelled at his ability of appearing whenever he was being spoken of or thought about. I hurried to meet him.

'I was just looking for you,' I said.

'Well, you found me. How's tricks?'

'It's on, the flat up town, I've seen it,' I began.

As I babbled on, his face assumed that look which appears when someone is not quite listening. When I glanced at him, he covered himself with a thin smile. His expression didn't deter me. Had I been less intent on convincing him, or a bit more sensitive, I might have seen that my enthusiasm was disturbing him. I'd never known him to be perplexed or fazed by anything. I steamrollered on about the apartment, its location, the potential effect of the Lea-Francis on the white-stockinged nurses who worked in the neighbourhood and upper-class crumpet in general, not to mention my plans for our careers in show business.

Eventually I ran out of gas. Lee, leaning against the satin ribbon bark of the big cherry tree, looked punch-drunk, a vacant smile playing on his lips.

'I think I'll have to pass on that one, me old china plate.' His voice was friendly, but the longing on his face betrayed the conflict sparked off within.

I didn't know at the time that he and his girlfriend had decided to tie the knot.

I was also unaware that Mum had convinced herself that she'd had her 'change of life'. When something started growing inside her, she'd become frightened and, suspecting the worst, taken herself off to Dr Brandreth.

Brandreth had reassured her. 'You're only pregnant again, Mrs Stamp.'

Mum was relieved, but none too happy. She had successfully reared four children and felt that motherhood was behind her. She enjoyed her bit of freedom and a new job behind the bar at the Iron Bridge Tavern. When I'd announced my decision to leave home, I'd added to her turmoil. I'd thought her reaction had been over the top at the time, but it wasn't until my Aunt Julie later set me straight that I learned of Mum's secret. By then I'd taken my bed and was well settled into West One. My reproaches at her for not sharing the news of her pregnancy with me didn't help. Frankly, I don't know where the newcomer would have been put had I not vacated the bedroom. When our new brother duly arrived, complete with dimple, black brows and slate-blue eyes, we all agreed that Ethel and Tom had saved the best until last. He was christened John Drew because he closely resembled the Irish line in our family.

Many years later, Mum told me that on the Saturday afternoon after I'd gone, Tom had sat her down and explained that even birds push their young out of the nest when they are old enough to fly. He assured her that, as a result of a proper upbringing, I could now stand on my own feet. Recently my sister confided to me that it wasn't only our mother's protectiveness that was threatened, but her pride as well. She believed the neighbours would naturally assume I'd left because it was 'so horrible at home'.

The day of my departure was calm but foggy: a real pea-souper. Baxter knew a fella with a small van who collected my bed and a few odds and ends. I walked out of 124 empty-handed, wearing my good suit. Mum came to the front door with me, as she had on countless other occasions, but as she kissed me and said the inevitable, 'Don't do anything I wouldn't do,' I understood that her clichés weren't banal at all, but just worn smooth by many years of conveying feelings she could not express in any other way. I felt tears well up. Suddenly, no longer at all confident, I turned and started to walk. The fog swirled about my hot eyes. I heard Mum say, 'Mind how you go, luv.' I just continued putting one foot in front of the other. It was like being blind. I could see my hand only when I put it right in front of my face. At every step I was tempted to turn back.

At the bottom of Greengate Hill I came upon a 699 bus. Its trolleys had come adrift and the conductress couldn't see well enough to pull them back down on to the power lines. All the lights were on inside the bus and the driver had lit a flare and placed it in the road to warn oncoming traffic. The scene was futuristic, like something out of an *Eagle* comic.

I caught the District Line to Mile End and it wasn't until I sat on the bench awaiting the Central Line to Oxford Circus that the thought came into my brain that I wouldn't be heading home any more on those eastbound trains. The westbound train I was waiting for was taking me 'home'.

I shouldn't ever have imagined that leaving 124 would be simple. That wonky little two-up, two-down in Chadwin Road remains deep in my psyche, like a spectral ship at rest on the ocean bed whose occasional shifts sends ripples through my sleeping hours. My attachment to my mother became stronger. At first, I felt self-conscious about accepting her invitation to take my laundry home; I was only too aware what a chore it was for her to wash and iron, especially iron. But, when Sunday lunch and laundry exchange became a firm ritual, a new link was forged.

One of the immediate advantages of my new freedom was the opportunity of eating exactly what I pleased when I pleased. This had never been possible at home as my 'finickity appetite' didn't fit in with Mum's tight budget. On my first evening of independence I remember coming home to 64 Harley Street from work and realising that I'd have to get my own dinner. On the way to the nearest grocer's (an American-style self-service supermarket), on the corner of New Cavendish Street and Marylebone High Street, I decided that peaches were what I fancied. I bought myself a large tin, took them home and ate the lot.

On the first Wednesday after we'd taken up residence, some of the group from the Method classes were invited over to see the place. There was the usual instant coffee and acting talk. Then Beth, who had a flair for reading cards and the like, suggested we hold a seance. George was enthusiastic and the rest of us went along with it. Beth wrote out all the letters of the alphabet along with a yes and no. George scissored them up and we placed them in order round the outside of our circular dining table. Somebody fetched a wine glass from the kitchen which was placed upside down in the middle of the table. We drew our seats up and Beth instructed each of us to rest a finger on the upturned bottom of the glass. When all our fingers were in position Beth asked, 'Are there any spirits present tonight?'

Almost immediately the glass moved towards the 'yes' paper. It was as though one of us was pushing or pulling the glass. It was obvious that we all had this impression. There was giggling and some of us removed our fingers from the glass. Beth told us that was how it always felt and, after we'd reassured one another that nobody was cheating, the seance was resumed. When asked to identify itself the spirit spelled out the name Guy de Maupassant. Asked whom the message was for, the glass moved directly to me. The message was then spelled out: 'Succeed yourself in order to succeed.' Nobody, including me, really understood this, and amidst a lot of speculation the seance broke up.

A month later a well-spoken girl joined the Method classes. She was pretty and had the shapely legs of a child ballet dancer who has stopped training. She was named Catherine. Although my taste in girls changed frequently, I was then going through a phase of being interested in muscular legs, so I made sure that she was included in the after-class soirées.

One evening, she in turn invited us all back to the flat which she shared with a girlfriend towards the end of the Northern Line. During the journey to Catherine's digs in Balham, I was a bit preoccupied, working out how I could get to know those legs more intimately.

We arrived at the semi-detached where Catherine lived and festooned ourselves around the bedsit with mugs of coffee. While I was perched on the side of Catherine's bed, I kicked into a plate which had been pushed underneath. Retrieving it to see whether I'd done any damage, I discovered two egg cups with broken egg shells and the remains of a long-past snack. That temporarily quelled my ardour.

During the perennial discussion on the merits of Method acting as opposed to the more traditional techniques, I was banging on, typical of someone who doesn't know much, when Catherine suddenly started to tear into me. I gathered I must have hit a nerve. She really berated me, accusing me of being a joke and not taking the business seriously. In answer to my request that she be more specific, she attacked my posture (which was apparently 'non-existent') and then opened me up with the cutting remark, 'And your voice . . . If you think you can get to act anywhere with that, you won't even get past the door – well, perhaps, if they're looking for lorry drivers!'

It didn't improve the relationship and it ended the conversation.

It was the typecasting that gave me pause, otherwise I might have dismissed the remark as typical of someone with a cut-glass voice and grubby habits. I hadn't embarked on this journey to play lorry drivers. Baxter had stayed uncharacteristically quiet during this tirade. We were both moody on the way home.

The following evening I broached the subject with him. We had a favourite bench in Regent's Park where we sat and watched the ducks. The park was usually empty of all but locals by seven o'clock and we often sat around until after dark.

Still smarting from Catherine's remarks, I said, 'What do you think about last night, Dave?'

'Well, I think she'd be a handful, probably squeeze the life outa ya with those Scotch eggs!'

'I was thinking about her comments, on my voice and stuff.'

'Yeah, made me wince. I never gave it a thought before, but I talk the same as you. I felt a bit like a leper.'

'It hadn't occurred to me, either. I'm sure Dean never had elocution, Brando neither.'

'That's America, though. It don't matter there. Perhaps we should take it up with George. You know, he's been in rep, done theatre.'

George was currently out of work, or 'resting', as he liked to call it. He was a packer at Liberty's, preferring to do menial work that wouldn't stop him attending auditions if and when they came up. He was endowed with the rare ability to see things from almost every point of view, and what Baxter and I gathered from his response was that Britain, unlike America, had a tradition of learning stagecraft in the theatre before even trying for film or TV. Nobody considered you at all if you hadn't done stage work. You couldn't get into Equity without a work contract. You couldn't get a job without an agent. No agent would represent you unless he'd seen you perform in the theatre and you couldn't land roles in the theatre without an Equity ticket. In fact, it was a closed-shop union. In George's view, no English agent knew his arse from his elbow, and if Dean, Clift and Brando had presented themselves at any London agency they would have been told, 'Let me know when you're in something.' George suggested that if we didn't believe him we should write to a few agents and find out for ourselves. We did – names withheld to protect the innocent. It was true.

The final conclusion we came to during our once-a-week Saturday cleaning blitz was that a would-be straight actor had to start at the bottom, as an oily rag in weekly provincial rep. These repertory companies, even in the farthest-flung provinces, took only young actors who had completed courses at recognised drama schools. It was clear where we should be concentrating our energies.

We were shattered. I asked George what he was doing at the Method school if he'd already been through this rep palaver, and it transpired that, not having made any headway in London after the provincial circuit, he'd hoped that the newstyle training might open avenues. I don't think George had actually been to drama school. He often referred to the theatre at Colchester which I assumed was his local theatre where he had started as a call boy or something and, although I wasn't absolutely certain about George's provenance, I didn't want to delve too deeply just in case he couldn't back up his stories. He was, no matter how tenuous, my only connection with the world of which I longed to become a part.

Baxter and I had nothing against the Royal Academy of Dramatic Art (RADA) or any of the other big schools, but their prices put them completely beyond our reach. Their annual fees were more than my entire salary and, as they offered only full-time courses, we would have had to work all night to study all day!

Our hopes were lifted when George said that RADA awarded scholarships. He suggested that we write off for the various syllabuses. We bought a copy of *Contact*, the theatrical directory, and wrote off to all the schools. It wasn't long before smart little booklets began arriving in the morning post. The big three were RADA, the London Academy of Music and Dramatic Art (LAMDA), and Central. Although George rated it highest, we scrubbed Central immediately because its course lasted three years whereas the others offered two-year courses.

Along with RADA, LAMDA and Central was another, smaller outfit called the Webber Douglas Academy of Dramatic Art. I pored over all the pamphlets as if my life depended on it, and, eventually, right at the end of the Webber Douglas literature I found the following paragraph: 'The Amehurst Webber Memorial Scholarship. This biannual scholarship is awarded to students of outstanding ability and insufficient funds.'

I certainly didn't have any strong opinions about my outstanding ability, but I definitely qualified on the second count. However, I wasn't sure that I had the front even to try for it. 'Outstanding ability' was a harrowing phrase.

Four
Increasing the Need

B axter discovered that all the English counties offered scholarship facilities and grants. I applied from the Chadwin Road address and he applied from Harley Street so that we wouldn't clash if each district awarded only one grant. When I collected the forms from West Ham County Council, it turned out that my dad's salary, although it never exceeded £12 a week, was more than double the figure which would have made me eligible for help.

Baxter fared rather better with his forms. I think his father was dead; he never really said. Whatever he told the authorities, he qualified for assistance, and he was given a special audition before a panel which assessed his abilities. He must have done well, because he was told that subject to passing the drama school's own audition – he'd set his heart on LAMDA – he would be awarded a grant.

I was delighted for him but I felt a bit in the dumps myself. All that was left for me was to try for the Webber Douglas scholarship. I wrote and received a reply almost straight away. I was asked to prepare two pieces of my choice: one classical, one modern. I would be tested in July for the term starting in September.

Knowing this prize wouldn't be a cakewalk, both George and Baxter started to give me back-up. George took responsibility for the classical piece and scoured his complete works of Shakespeare for a suitable speech. Baxter hung around French's, which stocked copies of almost every play ever written, looking for inspiration.

George finally decided on Romeo's death speech which he felt hadn't been 'done to death' because most students were so over-awed by it. In his opinion, the speech wasn't as difficult as it appeared, and offered lots of opportunities for movement around the stage which was a definite advantage. He told me to learn my lines before offering me any more advice.

43

'Learning the words is really the first and last of acting,' he said. It didn't make much sense to me at the time, but I took it on faith. Later, I was glad I did.

George explained to me that at an audition a student was allowed the use of two chairs and even if they were not already onstage it was perfectly all right to request them. We pushed the sofa, which divided the living-room, nearer the fireplace. In the rehearsal space we'd created George placed two chairs to represent the tomb on which Romeo finds Juliet whom he believes to be dead. George instructed me to think of the sofa as the footlights, and he positioned himself on the other side of it.

Had he not been so set on performing, George would have been a good director. My sudden interest in the more traditional aspects of acting, plus the fact that I had turned to him for guidance, released a fury of enthusiasm in him that I couldn't match. The archaic language; the rhythms, sometimes poetic, sometimes prosaic; and the precise points of in-breath necessary to read a phrase correctly while also remembering the text presented such a mass of problems that my brain frequently jammed up. I would stare at the lines for hours without taking in a word.

George's support never faltered. 'You don't have to be perfect; you're a student! You're going there to learn how to do it, but if you want the scholarship you have to be better than all the others.'

My depressions and mental blocks were partly due to the fact that Shakespeare took me right back to the hopelessness I had always felt at Plaistow Grammar. Everything at which I had failed so abysmally was there in front of me again, this time barring me from something I really wanted.

One evening, when I was tearing my hair out with frustration, trying to make more room in my head, George said, 'You know, Terence, this business is hard. It's so frightening to get up there knowing all the things that can go wrong, and at the same time make it appear easy, that the need has to be greater than the fear. Have you ever been up there in front of an audience, felt it slipping and not been able to control it?'

I told him about the last act of the East Ham Dramatic and Choral Society's production of *The Sacred Flame*. It was my début on stage, and I'd played a 65-year-old colonel. We'd given a public dress rehearsal in front of the Deaf, Dumb and Blind Society. On the first night, I hadn't been doing too badly, but I did everything wrong except fall off the stage. Just when I'd begun to see the end, it somehow all came apart.

He said, 'And that was for an amateur group, right? You can imagine what it would be like on a real first night, with press, the whole shebang!'

We giggled at the enormity of it.

I was now employed at Mark Fawdry's, a small advertising outfit with first-floor offices and a studio in Hanover Street. Of all the places I'd worked, this was by far the nicest, and that applied to all the staff including the boss. I worked in the art department with an artist called Pat, a young married man with a beard and a motor-bike on which he sometimes took me for a spin. There was also an older woman in the office, who looked like a sort of Miss Marple and who wrote short stories for women's magazines in her spare time. She encouraged me to try my hand at it, typing up my efforts and sending them off to the magazines which published hers, but I never had anything accepted. I stayed at Fawdry's longer than anywhere else and was doing all the typography and some of the visualising when I moved to Harley Street. The offices were so close that I didn't have to get up until nine o'clock. Nobody really worried when I arrived as long as the work was done on time. All in all it was my best moment in the ad. game.

I had been seeing a girl I'd met on the Piccadilly Line, with the wonderful name of Devina. She had dark hair, dark eyes and one of those marshmallow mouths that is hard to resist in any climate. Her parents were Roman Catholics with set ideas about pre-marital sex which she shared, but I enjoyed her company and had a lot of fun trying to change her views. Just before I'd left home this relationship had hit a watershed. She must have understood that I had other things on my mind than settling down, and I finally accepted that she couldn't give herself to me without the Pope's blessing. We tried to stop seeing one another, but it was too tempting. I suppose we both kept thinking that just one more time would change the other's attitude.

One day, after a rehearsal with George, at the end of which I'd seriously contemplated giving up the whole bloody acting thing and getting rid of the headache, I was at work in the studio at Mark Fawdry's, using the Grant Projector to scale down artwork to fit a new format for a scam to snare a hot-water bottle account. I was so engrossed that I'd completely forgotten about time and lunch until that empty feeling came on close to four o'clock. I nipped out to a snack place which snuggled in the bend of a narrow street opposite the studio. It was a warm afternoon and I left my jacket on the back of my chair and went across the road in my shirtsleeves.

I ordered two toasted buttered buns and coffee made with milk and went to sit by the window where a table-cum-shelf ran around the walls like a layout for an electric train set. Those buns really hit the spot! The waitress had rescued them from the grill at precisely the right moment before they could have been termed 'burnt'. Most people call 'burnt' what I call 'well done'. I've had these cravings for black toast ever since I had my appendix removed and, although you would think it the easiest thing in the gastronomic world to scorch a bit of toast, it actually requires a toast maker who either has the same addiction or who is devoted to a partner with similar cravings. Anyway, the buns that day came up roses, and the coffee, albeit instant, was made with a generous enough helping to cut the fatigue without wiring up the system.

I was not up, not down. The sunlight coming through the window on to my arm glanced the hairs above my wrist and gave them a shine. Into my brain came George's words, 'need it more', followed by 'increase your need'. My forearm was warm as it rested on the red patterned oilcloth of the shelf. People were walking down Pollen Street, too narrow except for the most fearless of drivers. Inside the snack bar the chromium silver urn gave its friendly hiss. All the sounds seemed to match the stillness in my head. 'Increase your need.' I ordered another coffee.

It took me a while to work out the implications. When I'd sorted out my priorities, I asked the boss at Fawdry's to look for someone to replace me, and stopped pestering the delicious Devina. I lived for as long as I could on the money I had put by, rehearsing the audition speeches by myself when the flat was empty. I told anyone who asked that I was a resting actor, just to get used to hearing it.

When the cash ran out I took a morning job in a small hotel in Nottingham Street which housed the patients of a nearby plastic surgeon while they recuperated. My first task of the day was to deliver breakfast trays to the twelve bedrooms. As soon as the inmates had eaten, the husband of the proprietress and I cleaned the rooms and made the beds. I had some bizarre encounters with recovering guests, particularly one young gent who repeatedly took it upon himself to have his ears reshaped, first one then the other and so on, in an effort to achieve a matching pair.

Baxter found me a comedy piece. I don't recall which play it was from but it was a speech given by a character who was one of a new breed of TV executives. The opening line was: 'We in TV . . . ' I thought it might be funny to say it in a sort of Ian Carmichael voice. Baxter invented a silly walk to match the voice which I went straight into as I spoke the first line. Baxter was intrigued by comedy. His serious approach to it rather took me aback, but I wound up working as hard on the light piece as I did on the classical. He reckoned that one should always be on the look-out for a laugh; it was amazing what a giggle could unlock. He told me that he had raised laughs from the battery of judges at the county audition not so much with his set pieces, but with the way he answered their questions when they interviewed him afterwards. Lee had always told me he had laughed more girls into bed than he'd had hot dinners, and my dad found humorous solutions for most of life's problems, so I wasn't unaware of the magic.

Viewing nerve-racking situations in a comic light was something which I took up with Baxter one evening when I met him from work. He had a temporary job at the offices of 20th-Century Fox in Soho Square. He was far from thrilled with the restrictions of being in work and seemed pleased to air his views as we strolled through the crowds of evening commuters in Oxford Street. It was still a grand street then and it gave us a kick to buy our provisions from Littlewoods which we regarded as our local shop.

Baxter's theory about nerves was really that there was no theory. There wasn't a system that was applicable because everybody was different and attacks of nerves never struck anyone the same way twice. I discovered that one of the things that had drawn Baxter to acting was the sudden flush of energy he experienced on stage – 'the pump' he called it. If it hit him right it catapulted him into a different dimension which had more time: everything around him in slow motion and he could move faster than others without appearing to do so. (I once met a master thief who wasn't a stranger to this condition. He used the same word – 'pump' – to describe what happened when he forced an entry with intent. He put one hand under his armpit and pumped his other arm against it in order to convey the sensation.)

Baxter was interested in the phenomenon which he saw as high-octane energy and he looked for ways of directing it at will. He advised me to apply for an audition at another school as a run-up to the Webber Douglas test. I told him of the idea I'd had to 'increase my need'.

He prodded my arm with one of his bony fingers. 'Yeah, that's great, like a samurai! But do yourself a flavour. Have a try-out first.' He shook his head at my apparent rashness. 'Come on, Tojo, let's see if we can scrounge a doughnut.'

My independence from an office job was hardly a release into Elysian fields, free from all care. Indeed, having so much time on my hands, I found I succumbed to a form of nostalgia that welled up whenever I thought of my mother. I soon realised that the coltish beauties who went with my new independence didn't know one end of a saucepan from another. My Sunday lunch visits to Chadwin Road became a regular event. I found myself repeating rituals that we'd had when I lived at home. My legs now easily stretched the width of the scullery door frame as I lounged watching Mum parboil the spuds before roasting them. On most Sundays I would repeat my boyhood task of expertly whisking the cold custard mix into the saucepan of rising hot milk, courting Ethel's appreciative glances.

We were closer than ever now I was living away from home. I saw more clearly the self-consciousness of her expression as she removed her steamed-up spectacles to give them a rub. She would return my thoughts with a myopic smile of her vulnerable eyes. So close was I to her during these unspoken contacts that it took all my willpower to stop myself clutching her sad hands and sharing every one of my plans and dreams. I longed to feel that flow of energy filling me with confidence. I would often move and stand with my back pressed against the door to the yard, imitating the position I'd held when she had bullied and tutored me to recite the poem that had so terrified me at primary school – 'You've heard about the wooden horse, the Wooden Horse of Troy?' breath 'And how the silly Trojans laughed and clapped their hands with joy' breath. I remembered my ten out of ten mark and felt the cross-frets against my back as though the duplication of sensation would fill me with the certainty she'd given me ten years before. I never spoke to her about my feelings. I ate her incomparable roast lunches and took heart in knowing that my plans included her just as much as me. Somehow it would all come right, and surprise us both.

Five
Dragon

The husband at the hotel where I worked was Polish. Although he had many of the characteristics of a man whose wife holds the purse strings, the basement kitchen was his domain. When our chores were finished we often had that part of the house to ourselves; his wife always stayed in bed late. He would make us very strong coffee and talk about the old country. I would lean back in my chair and study his collection of sausages which decorated the ceiling like a hanging garden, waiting for the moment when the caffeine would lift my head off.

I noticed that he was in pretty good shape and asked him about it. He told me that in his youth he'd been a gymnast and had stayed in trim out of habit.

'I think it helps the brain if the body is good. God knows, I need it around here,' he said, looking up towards the ceiling.

It was a notion I hadn't come across before, and as the Saturday afternoon stretched luxuriously before me (I had repeated both my speeches half a dozen times in my head while cleaning the loos) I drew him out a bit.

'When young, everything good, no problem, no think. Strength for everything. Me, because my father, God rest his soul, see I am strong boy, start me on ropes and horses,' he mimed gym equipment, 'because I learn quick, want to please my father, I become good, train for Poland.'

'For Poland! Wow!'

'No matter, competition not good, but I have good teacher, teach me not just muscles but stretch also. I practise because I like, even when competition stop. I notice others my age, same class at school, become slow, less interested in "how's your father". Not me, plenty lead in pencil! Also same here in England when I come.'

He leaned back in his chair, swivelling his head and looking me over.

'You smart boy, slim, good shape. Your father make you train?'

'No, he wanted me to box, but I didn't like it.'

'So what you do?'

'Nothing much. I used to play table-tennis.'

'You should do something, now while body young, get used to it. Like a horse. Start training young.'

'Yeah.'

'How much you weigh?'

'I don't know.'

'Let's go. You got five minutes?'

He unhooked a dusty sausage from the ceiling and put it into his coat pocket. I was about to tell him it wasn't good to carry anything bulky in a jacket, but his old tweed looked as if it had carried more than one baloney in its day.

We walked round the corner to a building in Paddington Street that I hadn't really noticed before. I saw that it was an old school, of the same period and design as Faraday junior in Holborn Road but on a smaller scale.

The Pole led the way downstairs into a full-sized gymnasium where a few guys were working out. Watching them was an older man with a lean and hard physique. He came over to us as we entered.

'This is guvnor,' the Pole said. 'This is young friend.'

'Terence,' I said, shaking the firm hand.

The baloney also exchanged hands.

'He would like to get into shape, has big test at acting school,' said my sponsor.

'Ah, actor,' said the guvnor.

'Going to be,' I said.

'Good.' He appraised me. 'Good for actor to be fit. Actors not fit now, but in the old days part of training.'

'I don't want to get big,' I said indicating my shoulders.

The two older men looked at each other and smiled.

'No,' said the guvnor, 'you won't get big here,' another sly smile at the sausage bearer, 'just long – and hard!'

'If you don't fall out.' The Pole grinned proudly.

The guvnor smiled at his chum's English. 'He means "back out". You come twice a week, Tuesday and Friday. Other days you practise by yourself. When is your test?'

'July.' I was wondering what I'd let myself in for.

'It's April now. Yes, by July I give you a routine. You won't need to come any more.'

'What – er – how much?'

'No cost for you. Friend of his, friend of mine. No cost for people who work. Only people who come here not to work pay.'

'Shall I start now?'

'No, we take your weight, height. Today is Saturday, you think about it. Come on Tuesday, this time.' He looked at his wristwatch. 'If you want we start then.'

'OK. That's a date.'

'No, think about it over the weekend. If you decide to start, no good backing out later. Waste of my time, OK?'

'OK.'

He took me over to the upright scale with weights, the same as the one at school. I slipped off my shoes and climbed on to the platform.

'Eleven stone and five pounds,' said the guvnor. 'Allow a pound for clothes, eleven four.'

He reached up, extended the metal measure and brought it down on to the top of my head. I stretched to my full height.

'Exactly six foot.'

'What! Let's have a look at that.'

It was true: the measure read six foot.

I used the time between Saturday and Tuesday to pump some information from the Pole. I wanted to know more about the guvnor. It seemed that he was originally from Yugoslavia. His real name was unpronounceable, but he was known to his friends as Dragon. Pronounced 'dra-gone', it translated as 'dear', rather than 'dragon' as I had hoped. He was older than he looked and had in his youth been something of a master with the sabre. It was rumoured that he had written a book about his system of physical culture, but he would neither confirm nor deny this. My employer had met him in a food shop which specialised in dried mushrooms and the foul-smelling sausage that aged in the basement kitchen of the hotel. He wouldn't tell me anything much about Dragon's system, explaining that the Yugoslav taught everybody differently.

At the hotel we changed the bedding of the regulars on Tuesdays; even so I finished my cleaning in record time. I hadn't any kit other than my table-tennis shorts which Mum had cut down from an old pair of trousers, a singlet and my plimsolls which I had blancoed for the occasion. The outfit had always stood me in good stead during the nightmarish dancing lessons we'd had at school.

I arrived straight from work to find the gym empty. I waited a while and then went out to have a tea in Marylebone Lane. When I returned Dragon was waiting.

'You are late.'

'I arrived at one-thirty. You weren't here so I went for a walk.'

'On Saturday I said "this time". It was two o'clock.'

I said, 'I'm sorry.'

'OK. This time OK. You must learn to take me precisely. Culture of the abdomen is a very precise business.'

'Yes.'

'You have your training clothes? Good. Get changed in the weigh-in room and we'll start.'

When I appeared in my outfit he looked a little dismayed. 'You don't have a tracksuit?'

I shook my head.

Dragon smiled. 'No sweat. I have one you can borrow.' He pulled a two-piece, navy blue, out of his holdall. 'Jump into that. Leave your underpants and socks on. We don't need shoes here.'

The suit felt warm as I put it on; it couldn't have been a better fit. Pure cotton, slightly fleecy on the inside, the top had a metal zip all the way up the front so that it could be zipped and rolled over like a polo collar or left slightly undone like a traditional windcheater. Both ankles had zips which gathered the legs in without the restriction of elastic. It was the best tracksuit I'd ever seen. Even my old table-tennis idol, Ray Dorkin, hadn't had one like this.

When I came out, dressed to kill, Dragon was standing in front of a long mirror which ran all along one wall of the gymnasium. As I joined him, I couldn't resist looking at my reflection and noticing how the suit had changed my appearance.

Dragon caught my glance. 'Vanity not bad for exercise. Can be used intelligently. You see, the brain remembers that it hurts before it feels good. Influence the person to do nothing, allows the body to become lazy. Vanity is good because it gives the brain positive objective, allows brain to help the body. You understand?'

'I think so.'

'Good. Here we work with the mirror, so you can see your position. Important you keep balanced. Straight. Often we think we are straight, when in fact we are crooked. In class I tell you when you are straight and you remember when you are on your own.'

'Right.'

'You think you are straight now, but your head is on crooked, like a psychopath.' He held my head and turned me to face the mirror. He was right: my head was crooked. 'This is chronic condition. You have this for a long time. Are you a psychopath?'

I shrugged my shoulders.

'OK. You must work hard to keep head on straight, very important. Crooked head leads to crooked breathing. Every breath has influence but uneven breath for long periods makes you off-centre. You must struggle with this – promise?'

'I'll try.'

'Promise.' He looked me evenly in the eyes.

'I promise.'

'Good. Promise have power. Like wish have power also.'

I nodded.

'Today we do feet. My culture is primarily the abdomen but we start with feet because we make contact with ground through the feet. We gather energy from the earth through our feet.'

'What?'

'We discuss later. For this time remember if we don't stand right, nothing right – not like animals for a purpose. We are upright, and this big advantage we don't use. Let me see your feet, please.'

I took off my socks. 'I've had trouble with them,' I said.

'I know.'

We sat on the floor and he examined my feet.

I said, 'I can never seem to get a pair of shoes that are really comfortable.'

'One is too tight, or one too big?'

'That's right. That's exactly right.'

'That's because shoes are pair, and your feet are not.'

'Come again?'

'Don't worry, not unusual. Most people's feet are a bit different, but your right is much bigger. Are you left-handed?'

'Yes, I am,' I said.

'And right-footed?'

'Yes.'

'When you have enough money you have shoes made. Find a good man. Czechs are best. Not cheap, but a bargain for you.'

I remembered seeing those little shops in St James's that made shoes to measure. I'd always been intrigued by them. I began to think old Dragon was amazing.

'These feet you have are good feet. They are weak because they have low energy and this joint is frail.'

He bent my toes under so that a third set of knuckles appeared like a fist.

'Ouch!'

'This foot falls in, will cause knee problems if not corrected, but potential is good. Now we talk how foot should be placed on the ground. Later I give you exercise to do at home. OK, stand up.'

I was suddenly aware of a great elegance and pride in the way he placed his feet: a spring in every step.

'Today I teach you what I call the melting foot. Foot covers the ground like water; it takes the shape it rests on. The moment it takes the weight the foot becomes steady, but yielding, like ice ready to melt; so water first. Heel contacts the ground like this.' He placed his heel to demonstrate. 'Then we position the foot on the ground along its outside edge until we reach the pad where the little toe joins the foot. We try to feel the pad under each toe until the pad under the big toe is grounded. Okey doke, now other foot. Heel, outside rim, little toe, across to big toe.'

We walked in slow motion towards the mirror, and then round the outside of the gym, with me struggling to get my feet grounded on all three points and Dragon encouraging me to try feeling the wooden parquet blocks which covered the floor.

Soon I became tired and I stopped.

He said, 'Feet are strong, remember that. Only brain is lazy. I'll show you something to freshen you up.'

From his bag he took a small cylindrical piece of wood, about a foot long. It looked as though it had been cut from a broom handle. He put it on the floor and, starting with his toes, trod over it inch by inch, so that when the wooden tube appeared at his heels every section of his sole had been massaged. He then repeated the procedure in reverse, moving his feet backwards over the stick. He did it twice more: once with his legs bowed, once knock-kneed.

Then it was my turn. If I thought the first time was painful, with my legs straight, the subsequent variations were excruciating, and I did it six times faster than he did. But when the throbbing in my feet stopped I didn't feel at all tired and we continued with the exercises. Dragon said I should do the two exercises at home; any broom handle would do. He told me the foot was a blueprint of the whole body and lines of energy from each major organ were connected to it. The exercises he'd shown me were like a quick all-over massage. He said that if I practised every day it wouldn't hurt at all. Then my feet would be strong, like a barefoot hunter.

When I left the gym it was getting dark and I was astonished to see it had gone six. Dragon had advised me not to speak to anybody about my training for the time being, and invited me to hang on to the tracksuit. I walked home trying to keep my attention on my feet. Nobody was in when I arrived so I boiled a kettle and a saucepan of water to top up the contents of the immersion heater and took a hot bath. My feet tingled in the water as I placed them precisely on the end of the tub.

The months flashed by. Dragon began to take over my life. I only ever saw him at the arranged times, twice a week, but his teachings spilled over so that even the most ordinary things became a matrix for his theories. I strengthened my knees by walking backwards upstairs. It took a bit of doing at first, like almost all of his exercises. He believed that the body itself was endowed with a fine intelligence. I trusted him and soon I was delivering my early-morning trays backwards, like someone from a Jacques Tati movie.

One day, as I was coming down the stone stairs to the gym, I found him waiting for me on the landing.

'Do you always look down at your feet?' he asked.

'I don't know. I've never thought about it,' I replied.

'You're in automatic, you mean?'

'I guess so.'

'Dangerous,' he said. 'Like a car without a driver. Go back up and come down again, looking straight ahead this time.'

I did so slowly.

'You can be more confident,' he said. 'Work the eyes in your feet the same as the eyes in your fingers.'

'How's that?'

'If you wake up in the night and reach out to get something you let the fingers find it. You can do the same with the toes. I'll show you. Tap the foot on each stair. Make a little song; the ears will keep you balanced. It's good to use your ears and give the eyes a rest.' He came tripping down like Gene Kelly, not looking down once.

He was often stern, but never pedantic. There was the business of my smoking, for example, about which he didn't comment until we started to do the stomach exercises. I noticed that the difference between my breathing and his was startling. He didn't chastise me, though. He said the body should be thought of as one's horse: you made it work the best you could. It was a delicate mechanism, and any bad habits it picked up had to be handled with care. Often a habit was like a bubble of air trapped under wallpaper: if smoothed out in one place, it would re-surface elsewhere. The problem with smoking was that it was intimately involved with the breath.

'Just think,' he said, 'you can survive without food for eighty to ninety days, without water for eight or nine days, but you can only make it without air for a few minutes. If it is that much more important . . . ' He shrugged his shoulders.

'Do you teach breathing?'

'No,' he said, 'it would take a very great person to teach breath.' He smiled. 'Though I did meet a lady once . . . but I was too young, too thick . . . No, with smoking, or any habit which has a hold on you, just wait and watch. There will come a moment when it is ready to give you up. Then you must let it go, and not be stupid.'

As we approached the try-out audition (I had taken Baxter's advice and registered for LAMDA) my lessons became more serious. I knew all the basic positions but, as soon as I was rippling through my set abdomen exercises, Dragon would make a little change that would leave me floundering. One Friday he demonstrated a lunge to stretch the hamstring in my leg and I caught a glimpse of the formidable swordsman he must have been.

He started inviting me to tea after class. The little pull-in for carmen a few doors away had put a table and chairs outside with Mediterranean optimism, and we would sit and watch the world go by. I often had to use my hands to lift my legs if I wanted to change position, so stiff was I before my hot bath. It was during our tea-time exchanges that Dragon's manner became intense. I figured that he was passing on to me as much as possible to boost my confidence. I wanted to hear everything; I was like a dry sponge. I asked him about his days as a fencer, but he said that we'd have that conversation when he knew me better. He gave me one of his long looks. There was an openness, an innocence about his eyes which was often at odds with the things he told me.

One day, he said, 'You would make a good swordsman.'

I shrugged off what I took to be a compliment.

'No, it's a fact, you have the eye. Still. And the body – unusual for an English.'

'How so?'

'You have a long back, which is not unusual, but you have long legs as well, and that is.'

'Well, if you want to teach me . . . '

'Ah!' was all he replied.

Six

Romeo From Bow

I attended the LAMDA audition in June. George and Baxter both wished me all the best before leaving for work, and I went through my paces alone in the flat before setting off down Harley Street to catch the 74 bus which would take me to the London Academy. On the bus I sat upstairs and went through both my audition speeches six times at speed and then once at performance pace. George's parting advice had been: 'Even if the proscenium collapses, don't dry!' Baxter had gripped my arms and whispered, 'Don't even think about the bloody emotions; they'll be there.' He'd given me his copy of *Sand and Foam* to read in case I had to wait, saying, 'It won't hurt for them to see you read decent stuff.'

I jumped off the bus just before Earls Court Road, walking the remaining few yards to the little theatre. I arrived early, a few minutes before eleven. I was directed to the wing of the theatre where the prompter sits, known as prompt side. A girl student asked me for copies of my speeches. She would be prompting me if I dried. I confessed that I hadn't brought them. First mistake. She asked me if I needed anything. I felt like a stiff drink. I asked for two chairs.

'Mr Stamp,' she announced and beckoned me on.

I was a bit let down by the auditorium, to tell the truth. It didn't even boast fixed upholstered seats like the Fairbairn Theatre, only a cluster of ordinary folding wooden chairs placed in uneven lines. There were three or four people sitting a few rows back. A youngish-looking guy appeared to be in charge.

'What have you got for us, Mr Stamp? The classical first, if you please.'

I placed my chairs, miming the prone Juliet (George's idea).

'Romeo's death speech,' I said and, without further ado, launched into it, my emotions exploding faster than you could say knife. At the end there was a silence. My pronunciation must have sounded pretty rough compared with the tones to which they were no doubt accustomed. I thought, Well, at least they haven't seen or heard Romeo as a barrow boy before.

After what felt like minutes the guy in charge said, 'Thank you – and your modern?'

I carried the chairs to the wings and returned to the centre of the stage. (George had said, 'Don't be frightened of holding centre stage – fill it. You never know when you'll be up there again.') After announcing my piece, I went over to the opposite prompt wing. I composed myself, took one step to attract their attention and then put my hands together in front of my face. I paused. I opened both hands and drew a full circle in the air. At the same time I bent my left leg and extended my right to take a low long step almost to middle stage. I did the voice and funny walk as rehearsed. It was a great success. I could hear them chuckling all the way through. Good old Baxter!

George and Baxter could not have been more pleased. I had to re-enact everything line by line, especially the bit when the guy had offered me a place. I'd been too embarrassed to confess to him that I didn't have the fees. George sat in the armchair, his black shoes pointing slightly inwards, a position his feet fell into when he was excited. He wanted to know about the reduction of fees and made me repeat the final conversation.

'He really said that? About a possible reduction? You're not pulling my leg?'

'No, I promise that's what he said.'

Baxter was standing by my bed, reflectively nibbling his thumbnail, and absent-mindedly repeating a dance step with his feet.

'They must have wanted you.' He was really interested to know all the details. His own try-out for LAMDA had been postponed due to a technicality over his grant. He couldn't start until the New Year so he was eager for any particulars I could recall. He wanted to know the size of the room, the area of the stage, the rake; everything.

George, always the pro, finally said, 'How d'you feel it went?' He sat with his jaw sticking out.

I thought about how he had shared the trauma of the preparation with me.

Baxter went to put on a kettle for tea.

'You know, man, the comedy went great, and I did our piece just like we planned.' I grinned. 'I was too frightened to forget the words.'

George covered his eyes. He should have told me about prompt copies.

'There was something,' I continued. 'You know that rush you get up there?'

He nodded. He dropped his arms between his knees, moving some of the low pile on the carpet, his head a fraction nearer to mine.

I drew back. Then I said, 'No, never mind.'

George snarled. 'Come on.'

'When I started, the rush hit me. You could have heard a pin drop, and then about halfway through . . . I guess around the "Tybalt, lies thou there?" bit . . . I had a feeling – it's hard to describe. I had this impulse to speed up. I wasn't going slow, I was on the metre, but I had this feeling to take it faster. I had to stop myself. I don't know . . . I mean, it all happened in a tenth of a second. Tell me, what d'you think?'

George considered. 'You lost 'em.'

'They wanted him, you egg! That's the main thing,' Baxter called through the hatch.

'Of course they wanted him, as a paying student! What he's aiming for is a scholarship, fees paid and an allowance. The Webber Douglas gig will be tougher. He'll be in straight competition with lots of others.'

'What to do?' Baxter mooched in with three mugs of tea.

'Has that bloody Gilly used all the hot water again?' George rasped, venting his disappointment that his choice of Romeo hadn't been one hundred per cent.

'I dunno. She's in, though; if she's played "Heartbreak Hotel" once she's played it fifty times,' Baxter added helpfully.

'I'm sorry, George, I didn't feel like Romeo. The Cockney accent sounded unreal. I know I'm going to study voice, and all that, but it grated a bit, you know.'

George thought for a minute. 'We could do something else. We've got a fortnight.'

'Yeah. Wot, though?'

Baxter stood up. 'I saw *Julius Caesar* last night. Brando's a great Mark Antony. He's got no voice to speak of, but he does it great.'

George snapped his fingers. 'That's it! "Friends, Romans, countrymen . . . " He's a working soldier.'

' "Lend me your ears." ' Baxter gave Marlon's rendition. 'You should go and see it, Tel,' he enthused.

'No,' said George. 'I'll go and see it. I'll see it tonight. We'll decide in the morning.'

I started rummaging around for the *Complete Works*.

Baxter said, 'Look at him. Took him months to learn Romeo. The screams were awful. Now, with one audition under his belt, he's goin' to sit down and learn Marcus Antonius while you're at the flicks.'

Down the passage 'Heartbreak Hotel' hit the turntable again.

George saw the movie and added to Baxter's enthusiasm for Brando's performance. He had spoken the verse beautifully, while bringing a wonderful emotional realism to the character. Gielgud was superb, of course, but, as Baxter was quick to demand, how would the great classical actor fare with Stanley Kowalski? They both urged me to see *Julius Caesar* as soon as I'd done the Webber Douglas audition.

George discovered that we had auspicious neighbours in the public eye living upstairs. The penthouse flat of 64 was rented to Glen Mason, Ronnie Carroll and, even more interesting to Baxter and me, a leggy blonde dancer from the Palladium. Although our basement didn't run to a television set, we knew both the celebrities from those black-and-white musical shows the BBC did in the Fifties, but the girl was a mystery. She slept late and we hardly ever saw her in the morning, but one afternoon I caught a glimpse of her. I guess it was a matinée day and she was between shows. She wore thick stage make-up and a loose white woollen dress over her tights. (The drabness of tights hadn't yet spread to the world outside showbiz and I was disappointed as I watched her climbing the stairs.) Even so, she had legs that just didn't quit.

We pumped Gilly for information about this disconcerting dancer. I don't think she welcomed the competition. She was untypically quiet, but George, who was around the house most and got on well with Gilly, discovered that the blonde wasn't attached to either singer. She was a relation, probably a niece, of our landlord. I suppose the girl must have been in her late twenties but to us the age difference was significant. Neither Baxter nor I had too much experience with older women and the dancer became an object of fascination and longing. We would hang around the ground-floor reception room after the last patient left, hoping to see her descend the staircase on her way to the theatre. Gradually the apartment at the top of the stairs began to represent a place somehow lofty and synonymous with success. We started to think of ways in which we could somehow incorporate this pad into our lives.

My body was noticeably hardening up. The exercises became less torturous, although in class Dragon always encouraged me to go beyond my limits. He told me about a Master of Sword whom he'd known in his early days at fencing academy. He'd been made to do exercises and movements that seemed totally superfluous, and always at the end of class when he was 'dead out on his feet'. Dragon had never understood this tendency but he liked and respected his master. He always tried his best, even though he thought some of the things he was asked to do were actually impossible. Then on one occasion he was in competition and had drawn an opponent superior to himself. He was completely exhausted before they were halfway through the fight. Desperate to finish the bout, to his own astonishment he found himself performing completely unorthodox bladework with a ferocity that reduced his opponent to a shambling amateur. In that moment he understood his master's 'craziness'. When his teacher died nobody could fill his shoes. Dragon had never met another who could work him to such a pitch and enable him to 'step down to his best'.

At the Tuesday lesson a few days before my scholarship try-out, Dragon was in a particularly sympathetic mood. I assumed that he was vibing me up for the big day, but something later occurred which made this lesson stick in my mind.

Dragon had always been adamant that all stretches for the stomach should be executed on the out-breath. I generally took a quick intake, managed as many repetitions as I could while the breath lasted, and in the pause inhaled once again. Dragon was keen to extend the time during which the body could go without breath and he taught one or two movements whereby the lungs were completely emptied. One exercise was to lift the rib-cage after exhaling, and then rotate the stomach muscles several times before inhaling.

'You'll never have bowel trouble if you can execute that properly,' he told me. (If only I had known this years ago I would have been saved from Mum's dreaded weekly dose of syrup of figs.) Dragon put great store in perfect elimination, saying that 90 per cent of all illnesses were caused when this vital function was less than perfect. I was instructed not to eat or drink anything for three hours before each class because this exercise could only be practised on an empty stomach.

Towards the end of class on that memorable Tuesday, I was standing with my legs bent and my hands on my knees trying the stomach rotation, when he suddenly smacked me on the head. It wasn't a blow but it was more than a tap.

I looked up, startled and gasping for air.

He said curtly, 'Your head is on crooked.'

Not knowing what to say, I didn't answer.

'You promised me to keep your head on straight!'

'I'm sorry,' I said. 'I was concentrating on rolling the stomach; it's not easy.'

'I know that,' he said, as I stood up. Then his expression softened. He took my head between his hands, gazed at me steadily and said, 'Look into my right eye.' I did. 'If your head is crooked and you lose it, you won't know where you are.'

I waited for him to go on but he was silent.

'I'm afraid I don't understand that.'

'It doesn't matter. Remember I told you! You must get used to being your own man. Nobody must be able to push you out of shape. When no one can pull you out of shape, you develop the smiling forehead.' Then he grinned. 'By the way, you were right about that theory of energy following thought . . . via the breath! When a thought is attached to the breath, and breathing is pictured as a swing, then that thought reaches all the atoms of one's mind and body.'

When I reported for my lesson on Friday, nobody was there. I sat outside the café next door where I could see anyone who arrived. Dragon didn't come so I scrounged a piece of paper from the café manager and scribbled a note for him. I went back home and did my exercises there.

I had a little trouble getting to sleep that night but I woke early the next day feeling fine. George awoke soon afterwards and we went through the new speech together. We had tried it with a variety of moves but had settled on playing it almost stationary. I thought this would contrast well with the exaggerated style of the modern piece.

I wore my jeans, which weren't real Levi's but were broken down and didn't look too bad, and a navy-blue cotton turtleneck which Baxter lent me for the occasion. George said I needed to look good but not too well off. 'You haven't any money, so don't go in looking as though you have.'

I had never been to Gloucester Road before. I arrived for the Webber Douglas audition on the Piccadilly Line which shared the station with the District and Circle Lines. The Piccadilly half looked older. Commuters surfaced in ancient wheezy lifts which faltered several times as though on their last gasp. The doors banged open directly on to the street facing an imposing Victorian building called Bailey's Hotel. A raised triangle of floral beds stood between the station and the Gloucester Road, a wide thoroughfare which accommodated several bus routes. The pavements were generous in scale, having been laid before space became a luxury. Opposite the long side of Bailey's was a parade of shops, some with their original curved windows. They were welcoming and I walked across for a closer look, my table-tennis shoes feeling soft and strange on the cobbled surface. I passed a bakery, weakening for a second as the aroma of fresh bread and pastries wafted past my nostrils. I caught sight of my favourite kind of doughnut, the colour of a horse chestnut. I resisted the temptation, promising myself one on the return journey if I did well.

I crossed the road where the 49 buses turned the corner, passed a restaurant called Dino's with a sign saying 'Real Italian Cappuccinos', a neat row of mews houses off to the left, and, finally, a pub with wooden benches outside, right on the corner of Clareville

Street itself. I suppose I was making a mental list, as a badger would mark a new sett. I dared not think about it too much in case my notations should prove unnecessary.

The Chanticleer Theatre was only twenty yards from the corner. I could hear my dad, who always gave directions using public houses as landmarks, saying, 'Turn left at the Hereford Arms and it's barely a stone's throw on yer left.'

It was unlike any theatre I'd ever seen, squeezed between two buildings like a wedge of Cheddar. The more I saw of the place, the more I liked it. I thought, This is exactly where I'd love to spend two years of my life. It wasn't grand and austere like RADA on Gower Street, or a gateway to the Orient like LAMDA in Earls Court, where every Australian in London seemed to be bedded down for the night.

Clareville Street was a backwater, an eyebath for the city-weary who stumbled upon it between the bustle of South Kensington and Gloucester Road. The front gardens bore witness to loving care and the place had a calm as if it were populated by retired colonels who'd decided to leave a beautiful mark on the London landscape and pruned their roses with military precision. The houses past the Webber Douglas building had deep front gardens which gave the impression to traffic on the Gloucester Road that it was a cul-de-sac. I passed the theatre entrance and the body of the school before locating the main door.

I stood facing it for a moment, reading the name on the wall plate repeatedly. I looked up the six steep steps to the front door and then glanced down through the open windows of the now abandoned rehearsal rooms in the basement. Finding no further excuse to delay my ordeal, I took one of my mum's deep breaths and climbed the steps.

The school was on summer vacation. The reverberations from generations of trained voices had been put on hold and the hush from the street permeated the building. As I approached the general office, a middle-aged lady with iron-grey hair was busy sorting papers at a desk, and I was able to take in fragments of this new world before she looked up briskly. She gave me a kind smile as I told her my name. My voice sounded strange to me; it punctured the atmosphere. Introducing herself as Betty Carden, she ushered me down the wooden staircase which groaned in long-suffering protest. We passed through a door where I found the stage boards of the smallest prompt corner in the business under my feet. It was so small that I assumed it was the OP (opposite prompt) corner. As my only other backstage experience was limited to Fairbairn House and LAMDA, in both of which the prompt side was located stage right, I had assumed this was how all theatres were designed.

The stage was lit with a rehearsal light. I gave the handwritten copies of my speech to a Mrs Huxtable who clipped them to a board and placed it on a shelf sloping out of the wall like a lectern. She switched on a hooded wall light and walked through the curtain on to the stage. When she called me out, I followed. I was feeling self-conscious about the fact that the sleeves of Baxter's jumper were too short for me, but he had warned me to resist hitching them up. Oh well, in for a penny, I thought, as an odd cool descended from the top of my head, as though somebody had placed a tray of ice on it. I straightened myself automatically, imagining that I was balancing a book, and tried to make my way across the stage without tilting it off. I knew everything was going to be all right.

In my later career, I never did get to play all of Mark Antony. Apart from an enquiry by Tony Richardson for me to play Oberon in a Royal Court Sunday night special, my attempts at the classics were confined to drama school.

'Friends, Romans, countrymen' unleashed in me a kind of fury which I had trouble in abating and it was fortunate that I had to start my second piece stage left, because I was travelling at such a pace that had I exited right I might have brained myself. As it was I stopped just short of the stairs, gulped a few breaths, and turned to go back on stage. Perhaps it was something in the way I executed the turn, a quick, quick slow that reminded me of Herbert's School of Dancing in the Barking Road. Out of the blue, the voice of my old dance instructor, Herbert Saunders, came into my mind. The memory of his twang (slightly to the right of Frankie Howerd) was so distinct that without further thought I went into the comedy piece giving a full imitation of a voice which I hadn't heard in years.

A portly man in the centre stalls started to laugh immediately and was soon joined by the others in the group. When they all applauded at the end, I was so taken aback that I bowed, exited stage right, and walked straight into the wall. I returned on stage, feeling silly and flustered.

The portly man introduced himself as George Rossiter and proceeded to ask me a few questions. 'Did you have any help with your pieces?'

Without hesitation, a 'yes' came out of my mouth. Then I remembered George telling me, 'You're not supposed to be coached, so don't admit it, whatever you do.'

'I see, and who helped you?' I was silkily asked.

I remembered Baxter saying, 'Go for laughs if you can,' so I replied, 'Oh, the guy I share a flat with.'

'And what does he do?'

'He's a packer at Liberty's, Sir.'

Everybody in the stalls giggled. I knew I was back on course. I explained my financial situation, making it clear that I had no funds and would need all my fees paid and money to live on.

Mr Rossiter, who turned out to be the principal, explained that the bursary was a modest one and if awarded would fund me only £8 a month.

I thought, Well, that covers my share of the rent; I've only to eat and travel. That should do. I could walk to school if I had to.

Finally, they all thanked me for coming and Mr Rossiter said, 'We have to see two other applicants but, of those we've seen so far, I can tell you that you are the strongest contender. We will inform you as soon as we've made a decision.'

'When can I expect to hear?' I asked, trying to sound as if I had dozens of scholarships to choose between.

Mr Rossiter looked briefly around at the group and said, 'This afternoon. Will that be soon enough?'

I nodded.

'That will be fine, thank you.'

I thought, I've got this. I've bloody well got this.

I took off to buy my doughnut.

Mrs Huxtable rang at four-thirty and said that I had been awarded the Amehurst Webber Memorial Scholarship. It had been a unanimous decision. The award would commence on 22

September when I enrolled for the autumn term. Everything would be confirmed in writing.

A few weeks later I turned twenty. It was 1958. The Everly Brothers topped the British hit parade with 'All You Have to Do is Dream'.

The only cloud on my horizon was that Dragon had gone missing. On Tuesday when I reported to the gym, bursting with my good news, I was informed that Mr Horniman no longer rented the studio. I said I doubted his name was Horniman and gave a detailed description to the girl who organised the letting of the premises.

'Yes, that's him,' she said. 'Mr Horniman.'

I chased back to the hotel and took the matter up with my Polish chum.

He didn't seem at all put out. 'He often takes off like that. I shouldn't worry. You know your programme. He'll be back.'

'Yes,' I said. It suddenly felt dark. 'I didn't get to tell him that I won the scholarship.'

'Oh, he knew that, he told me weeks ago.'

'Weeks ago?'

'He said you had the mark on you.'

I left my cleaning job at the end of August. But I continued to stroll past the gymnasium in Paddington Street to see whether Dragon had returned. There was never any news. Eventually the school was closed and the building changed hands. I often wondered what gym classes at school might have been like if somebody like Dragon had taught us instead of Mr Priest.

One evening after a workout I was examining the tracksuit Dragon had given me when I discovered a faint outline just below the breast pocket where an emblem or badge had once been stitched. It set me wondering afresh about Dragon and his abrupt departure. It was many, many years before I understood how difficult it was to find a real teacher, and how easy the great ones made it to leave them. Strolling along Oxford Street or in that part of town, something he'd said would come into my mind, and I would straighten up and step out. I didn't want Dragon to come upon me out of shape.

Seven

The Scholar

That spring of 1958 something slotted into place and I felt ready to take on all comers. Having made the commitment to study acting full time, my life changed. I had followed my feelings, and I held my breath as events unfolded.

When I began at Webber Douglas and Baxter was still waiting to start at LAMDA, he and I became closer. He was impressed at the fact that I had gone for the scholarship and landed it. For the first time in our friendship I had taken the initiative. He was curious about what had gone on in my mind during the audition and made me go over everything time and time again. These discussions usually took place during long strolls when we aimlessly surveyed our patch, sometimes stopping for a coffee around St Christopher's Place where new tea salons were sprouting up like mushrooms. We usually wound up in Regent's Park where we hung out until the gates were closed.

One night, when it was almost dark, we made our way towards the park gate near the top of Harley Street and walked past a bank of wallflowers. Their scent was so overpowering that we stopped and kneeled on the grass to inhale their heavy aroma. The depths of the blooms smouldering in the dusky light reminded me of a Persian rug I'd seen in a window at Liberty's. I wondered if it might be possible to cultivate the flowers in ordered sections of varying shades to resemble a carpet.

We left the park and crossed over the main road into Harley Street. We were commenting on the fact that we never saw any locals after six o'clock. We decided that 64 must be the only building whose tenants were not in the medical profession.

At that moment I spotted a piece of string hanging down in front of a wide impressive door. I remarked on this to Baxter and we traced its knotted route right up to a top-floor window. It was as irresistible as a Heath Robinson illustration. We couldn't walk by without giving it a tug. Neither of us actually wanted to do the deed, and we finally compromised: I would pull the string while Baxter watched the window. I gave a couple of gentle tugs and nothing happened, so I pulled harder. Suddenly the string disappeared like magic. After a minute or so Baxter pointed to the front door and mimed running footsteps. Just before the door opened we heard a breathy feminine voice saying, 'Bobby, Bobby, you made it – goody.' The door was flung open to reveal a girl in her twenties, hair in disarray, wearing a baby-doll nightie.

For a moment nobody moved. Pushing Baxter in the chest, she said, 'Not you!' and slammed the door.

Baxter and I walked around the block giggling. When we passed the house a second time the string was once more in place.

I said, 'I'd love to know who Bobby is when he's out.'

'He's on night shift, whoever he is.'

When I started at Webber Douglas, or Webber D as it was known, my first discovery was the taboo about discussing film acting, or voicing any ambition to work in films. During the first week I didn't speak unless spoken to, a useful tip I'd picked up from my dad. Curiosity about 'the scholar' soon faded and I settled into student life. Nobody made any remarks about my accent. Gradually, I began to relax and look around me. I noticed that there was a definite hierarchy among the guys, and a lot of the girls were impossibly pretty. For the first few days I felt a little dizzy, being in such close proximity to so much physical beauty.

I soon discovered that George Rossiter was not only the principal but the owner of Webber D, and he ran it as a hobby. At most other schools a class would concentrate on one play a term, but at Webber Douglas each year's students performed several plays, rehearsing them simultaneously throughout the twelve-week term.

On the first day, I was sitting in the window-seat of the small commonroom facing Clareville Street, getting my bearings, when the cast lists were posted on the noticeboard. There were squeals from the cluster around the board as my fellow students discovered who was playing which roles. It struck me as odd that their main interest seemed to be in the classics.

Like me, all the first-termers were nervous and unsure of themselves, with the exception of a blond guy, a good three inches taller than me, called Stuart Hoyle, and a dark type named Michael da Costa, who was a born clown. The second-year students were self-assured with a kind of easy charm. They enjoyed physical contact and squeezed each other a lot.

Webber Douglas was different from the Method school in Dean Street by a long chalk. I had no inkling at the time that this pride of young lions at Webber D were just part of a wave which would gather and crash over the whole of Britain when the Sixties officially started. Michael Coles was the first from the top echelon to welcome me. Raw-boned, with a warm smile, he could flash energy across a room like a searchlight. He was later included in Kenneth Tynan's prestigious 'top ten young actors of the year' round-up for his West End début in *Progress to the Park*. Rick Jones was the one all the girls seemed to swoon over. He was a poet and balladeer. I was always overhearing girls telling him what a wonderful singing voice he had. I wondered why he didn't get into the music business straight away. Years later he formed the pop group Meal Ticket, writing and performing his own material. Steven Berkoff was a loner. Dressed in existential black, his big still eyes missed nothing. He never spoke much but he wasn't unfriendly. From the start I tried to catch the performances of another second-year student. She was a riot and her name Penelope Keith. But the queen in this hive of activity, and the girl most of the boys had a crush on, was a gamine with green eyes and a mop of hair Titian would have flipped over. Her name was Victoria Louise Eggar – until the day she saw Grace Kelly in *High Society* and transformed herself into Samantha.

A Midsummer Night's Dream was to be our Shakespeare play for the first term. My only experience of the *Dream* was a production I'd seen at Plaistow Grammar. I'd had such a thing about Hilary Lago who was playing Hermia that I'd been hardly aware of anything or anyone else. It didn't really come across to me how funny the lovers could be until I saw Peter Brook's famous 'trapeze' production many years later.

Our director was a Miss Lowry, one of the old school. At Webber D students were known either as cookies (look good straight on) or birds (best in profile). Helen Lowry was definitely a bird. The real difficulty in learning anything is finding a good teacher. I was lucky at Webber D: on the occasions that mattered, I was in the right place with the right company.

Helen Lowry marshalled us around the stage as if she were a general in charge of Dad's Army. I was cast as Lysander, one of the four lovers. A fellow called Christopher Gabriel played Demetrius; he was exactly the sort of chap you would cast as an equerry at the Palace. When he first spoke to me I thought he was pulling my leg. He sounded like he had a mouthful of marbles and I sounded like one of the Bisto Kids. Other actors in the play would turn away and walk upstage when we started delivering our lines.

I remember one piece of direction we received from Miss Lowry in the last act. At the moment when the spell is lifted from the lovers and they wake as if from a dream, she told us all to laugh.

'Say that line and then you all laugh.'

I wanted a motivation.

She said, 'Just do it.' She demonstrated. 'If you find it difficult to laugh onstage, just take a deep breath and start saying, "Ha ha ha".'

Of course, nobody else had trouble laughing watching Chris and me trying to negotiate this technique.

At the end-of-term performance we staggered through this epic, advance word of which had filled the auditorium. There were some classic performances: ex-showgirl Kim Carlton making her début as Titania and Kathy Breck whose 'Wall' I'll always remember. Chris and I, terrified at coming across like Laurel and Hardy, just tried to keep our tights up and get through our lines as quickly as possible. When we reached the part when the spell was lifted, we were so relieved that we laughed hysterically.

When giving us her criticisms the next day – notes, she called them – Miss Lowry, whose handbag was never short of a razor-blade, said, 'There you are, Terence. That laughter was the most spontaneous moment of your whole performance.'

Gloria Kindersley was the first girl at Webber D to take me up. One day we were gossiping together at a late-morning rehearsal and she invited me to lunch at her place.

'It's around the corner,' she said, 'in Chelsea.'

The Scholar

She cycled to school but as I'd left my bike with my brother in Plaistow, never dreaming that West End folks biked to work, we caught the tube at South Ken, one stop, to Sloane Square. Like Chelsea, Sloane Square was somewhere I'd never visited. As we crossed the square and I had my first glimpse of the King's Road, I was filled with a kind of exultation. It was another world, even further back in time than the Gloucester Road. It was as if a country village had been transported to London. There were Victorian bakery shops, their windows stuffed with cakes, the like of which I'd never seen, greengrocers with displays spilling out on to the pavement, boxes full of fruit and veg I'd only ever heard of. I could have stood there all day, but, not wanting to appear gauche, I pressed on with Gloria who was walking nonchalantly through the midday shoppers: some made-up and elegant, others in open sandals and shapeless frocks. All the men seemed to be wearing jeans, even those who were not so young. It was dazzling.

The explosion of the Sixties brought many wonderful changes, but one of the things it demolished for ever was the King's Road I saw that day. I felt like a king when I first sauntered along on my way to Gloria's home in Radnor Walk, and I rarely pass the corner baker's on Bywater Street, with their never-to-be-forgotten chocolate Swiss rolls, or one of the few remaining original establishments without thinking of that outing.

As we neared the Chelsea Potter, a landmark even then, Gloria said, 'What would you like for lunch?'

'Well, anything you got.' In those days Ethel's Sunday lunch was my only square meal of the week.

My heart and stomach sank when Gloria said, 'We haven't anything in the house but we can get something. What would you like?'

This was becoming embarrassing. I felt the outsides of my denim pockets, which were as flat as pancakes, save for the fare home: sixpence.

'I'm a bit short at the moment.'

'Oh, don't worry. I'll buy.'

'Have you money, then?'

'No, but I'll charge it.'

I supposed she meant 'on the slate' so I said, 'You've got an account in a shop near here?'

'Well, the family has lots. Now, where shall we go?'

First we went to the butcher's, opposite a shop called Thomas Crapper, Sanitary Engineers by Royal Appointment (something to tell my dad about), where Gloria bought chump chops and kidneys. She turned and looked at me from the counter. I was busy making designs with my foot in the sawdust. Now it was she who was embarrassed. For a second I thought she'd over-extended her credit. I had visions of my chops going back on to the slab, but then she asked, 'Can you cook?'

'Oh, sure,' I said. 'I can cook all right. You put it down and I'll fry it up.'

The Kindersley family house in Radnor Walk fulfilled all my expectations of an upper-crust home. Until then the only classy interiors I'd seen had been in movies. In a funny way there were many similarities with Mum and Dad's house in Chadwin Road. Everything was spotlessly clean and had that familiar worn-out look which gave the rooms a cosy, welcoming feel. There was even a settee with horse hair coming out in tufts through the splitting leather. I asked Gloria about some of the mats – rugs, she called them – which looked almost threadbare, and ready for the dustbin. She explained that they'd been in her family for years and she thought they were valuable. I realised that if you could afford good gear it lasted longer and could be considered an investment. When it grew old it became chic and you could sell it rather than throwing it away.

The rooms weren't big, but there were lots of floors and staircases sprouting off in all directions. Each landing had its own bathroom or lavatory. Gloria said it was the family's town house; her parents spent most of the time in the country.

I hadn't ever seen a kitchen like the one Gloria showed me. To my eyes it had everything and, despite Gloria's fears that there was no food at home, I could have survived for a fortnight on what was in the Kindersleys' enormous fridge. I soon had myself organised but couldn't find any lard to start the fry up. Gloria didn't understand what lard was, but, when I explained that it was what I used to fry food in, she told me to use butter or oil. (We never had butter at home. In fact, I'd become so conditioned to the taste of nationalised marge that when the War finished and they eventually got round to marketing different brands – Stork and the like – I couldn't eat them until Mum found me something called Echo which tasted familiar.) I was wary of cooking in oil, so I settled for butter although I winced a bit at the idea.

I think that lunch was one of the best I ever had, even if I say so myself. Gloria didn't do badly. She ate almost as much as me, and was quite taken with the fried bread, which I'd added as an afterthought, dropping two slices into the juices left by the chops, kidneys and tomatoes. She said she had never tasted anything like it.

The other person I teamed up with was Stuart Hoyle, the striking-looking guy whom I'd noticed on my first day at Webber D. He was about my age and had played Theseus in the *Dream*. He came from up north but was sharing a flat in nearby Walton Street with an older guy called Mike Jackson. The students at Webber D had quickly fallen into two categories: those who firmly believed they were preparing for a future in the theatre, and the drifters. Stuart Hoyle was definitely the former. He had a self-assurance which some called arrogance but which had instantly drawn me to him. His flatmate was a good deal older and he acted like Stuart's sponsor. He must have had a private source of income or an allowance because he didn't appear to have a job. He was in the habit of fixing snacks at their pair of rented rooms in Walton Street or taking Stuart out to dinner and, when he realised that Stuart and I got along, I was often included on these outings.

One evening Mike invited Stuart and me to have dinner with a friend of his, a journalist who was a bit of a cook and who lived in a little basement flat just off the King's Road.

When we arrived at about eight-thirty, there were already two men there; one of whom, the host, had a bad limp. Stuart and I figured that he probably had a false leg. We all sat around, the guy with the limp occasionally going into the little kitchen, but no food appeared and it was getting late. I hadn't eaten at all that day and was feeling ravenous. Just as I was beginning to give up hope, the food arrived and we gathered round the small dining table. It was obviously the main course, as each of us was given a large plate heaped with food: a thick pork chop and all the veg cooked together in some kind of sauce. It looked delicious and, boy, was I hungry! I cut myself a big piece of the pork, and prepared to wolf it down. As I lowered my head towards the food a powerful odour greeted me. Very powerful indeed, and thoroughly obnoxious. As unobtrusively as possible, I raised my head, closed my mouth and put my fork back on to the plate, glancing around to see how the others were reacting. They all seemed to be chomping away contentedly. I poked about on my plate, trying to scrape the sauce off the meat in an attempt to isolate the stench.

Eventually Mike noticed that I wasn't eating and asked me what was up. Feeling very self-conscious, I explained that I thought something was wrong with my helping. The others sampled my food and found nothing amiss. Then Mike said, 'It's the garlic. Don't you like garlic?'

I had to own up: I didn't know what garlic was. I'd only ever heard it mentioned on the radio on *Mrs Dale's Diary* and had wondered what it was.

Stuart forked my chop on to his plate. The guy with the limp looked in the kitchen for some cheese but came back empty-handed. The cupboard was bare. He was obviously hard up and had splashed out on buying the meat.

The next morning in class, when I asked Stuart how he could possibly eat something with a smell like that, he said he loved it and had heard it was sperm-producing. His breath was enough to curl your teeth. It was completely beyond me. It was ten years before I felt brave enough to try garlic again.

My major concern during those first few months was getting sufficient to eat. Baxter and George managed to bring some food home, but as they were on the breadline as well we existed mainly by eating beans on toast. Baxter invented an ingenious morning drink which we made by pouring hot water on to a spoon of jam. We used up all the old jars of jam and marmalade this way. But it was obvious that I couldn't go on scrounging meals from other students: there was already a rumour among the girls that I was anybody's for a three-minute egg. I would have to get a job.

After making some enquiries, I discovered that a few students at Webber D had jobs although it was frowned on by the staff.

The Scholar

One boy told me that he worked evenings at a theatre in the West End. He was a showman dresser which meant that he wasn't on the day staff and worked the shows only in the evening. For this kind of casual labour he was paid by the performance and didn't have to join the union. He earned close to £5 a week and paid no tax. In fact, the only problem was the midweek matinée which was at two-thirty every Wednesday when he was at school, so he'd had to find someone to cover for him. I asked him how he'd come by such a cushy number. He said he'd asked at the stage doors, telling them that he was a drama student looking for evening work. My best chance was to find a new show which was about to open and wasn't yet fully crewed.

The next day I saw a note pinned on the noticeboard in the commonroom: an invitation to the dress rehearsal of a new play at the Piccadilly Theatre. Equity members and drama students could attend free of charge. The play was about the Hungarian uprising and starred Emlyn Williams. I went. Before going in I walked round to the stage door and did my piece. The stage doorman was sympathetic and said, 'Look son, we're in a bit of a two and eight tonight, but I'll make a note of your name. Come back tomorrow about six and have a word with the stage manager.' The play wasn't up to much but I went back the next day and, to my delight, was given a job – as dresser in charge of the OP changing room. I didn't have to do much: I just had to have the costumes ready for whichever of the actors needed quick changes. It was good to be in the theatre and earning money, even if it was only as a dogsbody.

One night, one of the leading players, a Scandinavian named Mogens With, was unexpectedly taken ill and another actor I'd seen on TV as the Buccaneer went on at short notice. He was called Robert Shaw. The atmosphere was electric on his first night. The other members of the cast, Emlyn Williams and Stephen Murray included, were nervous for him but Shaw didn't put a foot wrong. I was very impressed. Not even he could save the play, however, and it closed a few weeks later.

Another play, a farce entitled *Hook, Line and Sinker*, starring Robert Morley and Joan Plowright, was set to open right away. I was asked if I'd like to continue to do the same kind of job. I did, and as the new show came in over a weekend I was free to hang about behind the scenes. I felt at home. It reminded me of the first time I'd assisted with a 'get in' at the theatre in Fairbairn House Boys' Club. One of those succinct theatrical terms, a 'get in' describes what happens when the finishing production 'wraps', usually packing and moving out after the Saturday night performance, and the new production gets in immediately. Speaking as a product of two working-class dynasties, I've rarely witnessed or been part of a more efficient job of work. It is more like an international football team than a gang of labourers, with each member searching for things to do.

Just before we broke up for the Christmas holidays, there was a rumour at Webber D that next term several classes of first-year students would be used for a production of *Othello*. Overnight this news became the main subject of gossip. I didn't know anything about the play except that its chief character was a big black bloke.

Stuart invited me for a coffee in the lunch-break and we sat at a table outside Dino's. It was cold outside, and the management didn't mind us not eating; as it was busy inside our order took a long time coming. Stuart didn't hang about. He started to tell me what was on his mind as soon as we sat down. He was excited and there were spots of colour in his normally sallow complexion. He repeatedly brushed away his long fair hair as it fell over his eyes.

He assumed that I'd heard about the forthcoming production and when he cottoned on to the fact that I knew next to nothing about the play he explained that there were two important male leads: Othello and his lieutenant Iago. Othello, a Moor, was usually played by an actor of some physical stature and Stuart was almost certain that he would be cast in the role because of his height. I mentioned Brian Coburn, another giant in our class, but Stuart brushed this suggestion aside.

'The important thing is that you get Iago,' he said. 'He's a really evil sonofabitch; it's an equally good part. When Richard Burton and John Neville played them at the Vic they swapped roles halfway through the run.'

I understood that it would be more fun if we were both in the production but I didn't see why Stuart was so het up about it. After the coffees had arrived, and we'd drunk them, the reason for his excitement came out: Mike Jackson, who had a few connections with showbiz, knew an agent. Stuart believed that if the production proved to be really good Mike would bring his agent chum along. I had to promise Stuart that I wouldn't repeat to anyone, not even Mike, what he'd just told me. It was against school regulations to invite professional theatre people to any play other than the 'show performance' at the end of the two-year course.

I was impressed, to say the least, by Stuart's forward thinking. He was already planning his launch into the business. I felt like a babe-in-arms compared to him. Of course, once he'd divulged his strategy, I couldn't fail to see the sense of it.

'Who is directing it?' I asked.

'I heard it's Peter Bucknell. He lives near the school. Supposed to be hot stuff.'

'Well, I'll keep my fingers crossed and hope for the best.'

'You could talk to Rossiter about it. After all, you're the scholar.' He laughed. His laugh was raucous, unlike the rest of him which was smooth and poised.

Over the Christmas holiday Mike Jackson gave what he called 'an evening'. He told us that Anthony Newley was going to drop by. I was looking forward to it. I'd admired Newley ever since I'd seen him as the Artful Dodger in David Lean's *Oliver Twist*. But he didn't show up and I began to have my doubts about Mr Jackson's connections.

There was a second-year student at Webber D named Patrick Scanlan, a looker with thick Elvis-type hair. He was the social cog in the school wheel. As well as hosting a number of get-togethers himself, he was a mine of inside information on where and when things were happening. I can count on one hand the parties I went to while at Webber D. At the first, given by Patrick, I met the Greens: Earl and his wife Denise. Earl was dark and saturnine – he was a convincing Richard III – and his wife, also dark, was from Israel. On this particular evening they wore matching turquoise Indian silk shirts which I coveted. As I was leaving I heard a girl's voice calling from a second-floor window. I looked round and saw a halo of red hair lit from behind by the bedroom light. She was leaning out of the window with her hands on the sill. It took me a moment to realise that she was yelling goodnight to me. That was the first time Samantha Eggar had the mind to speak to me.

Another party invitation obtained by Patrick was to a do in Portland Crescent. The only reason I went was because it was just up the road from Harley Street, which meant that I wouldn't have any problem getting home. I was also curious about what those grand buildings looked like inside. I wasn't disappointed. The party was in full swing when I arrived after the evening show at the Piccadilly. I nodded to the few people I knew, and then caught sight of Stuart in a group who were crouched down beside a gramophone on the floor. It was the usual box-type, with a lift-up lid and the amplifier at the front.

Stuart called out, 'Get a load of this. It's the *West Side Story* cast album. The show's just opened in London.'

I normally have to listen to a piece of music several times before it grabs me – that's if it's going to grab me at all. But this recording was different. It made such an impact on me that I knew I had to see the show. Or, better still, get involved with it as soon as possible.

Eight
On West Side

The next day I went round to the stage door of Her Majesty's Theatre between the afternoon and evening performances of *West Side Story*. Some of the stage crew were hanging about outside having a smoke. I asked one of them whether the stage manager was there.

'Mr Shardi? What do you want with him, son? I wouldn't bother him if I was you,' was the reply.

'Why, what's up?' I asked.

'The show's a nightmare; more cues in that prompt corner than half a dozen normal shows put together.'

'Sounds great.'

' 'Tis if you're in the house. What are you after?'

'Er – a job.'

'Can you work a lime?'

I had no idea what a lime was so I just shrugged confidently.

'Got a ticket?'

'Sure,' I lied.

'I'm Harry,' he said, 'carpenter. Vic, the chief spark, isn't around but they need someone up in the limes. Nip up now, I think there's a spark up there.' He pointed to the main stairs.

I knew that 'sparks' meant electricians and the ticket was probably a NATKE union card. Well, I'd face the National Association of Television, Theatrical and Kinematographic Employees when I came to it. I waited until my informant drifted away and then went to ask the stage doorman where the limes were.

'Lime box? Up them stairs as far as you can, then all the way down the passage. On yer right a little pass door, through there all the way and then a few steps up. That's yer limes.'

I thanked him. As I leapt up the stairs I passed the closed doors of the stars' dressing-rooms with the handwritten names of Don McKay, Chita Rivera and George Chakiris. The farther up I

93

went, the less private things became. On the next floor dressing-room doors were wide open, with their occupants lounging in the doorways, half in costume, half out. Trays of hamburgers, uneaten sandwiches, and clothes, all the colours of the rainbow, were strewn all over the shop. I wasn't in the West End; I was on Broadway.

The lime box, when I reached it, was just that: a box. It was built around four huge carbon arc lights, each the size of a cinema projector. In the room was a man in a lumpy old sweater engrossed in a book. I stood there, mesmerised by the four monsters. There was nowhere else to look. When the man eventually glanced up, he appeared perturbed to find me in his eyrie. We were right up over 'the gods'. Even at the Queen's Theatre, Poplar, with its nudey shows (when it was legal to have bare girls onstage but illegal for the naked beauties to move), I'd never been this high up.

I said, 'Hi.'

He said, 'Hello.' He looked the type who would smoke a pipe and he did. He brought the pipe out of his pocket and put it unlit into his mouth.

I thought, This fella's an artist; I can't flannel him.

'I heard you need someone to work a lime.'

'Can you start tonight?'

I was completely taken aback. I said, 'I could, but I'd have to get someone to cover for me at the 'Dilly.'

He scrutinised me. 'I didn't know they were using limes.'

'They're not. I'm on the stage.'

'OK.' He smiled, pleased that he'd been right about his hunch.

'I can start Monday. I'd love to do the show, but I should tell you I don't know much about these chaps.' I tapped the arc nearest to me.

''S'no problem. What's your name?'

'Terence – Terry.'

'OK, Terry, you get here Monday 'bout quarter to seven. I'll teach you. Eyes all right?'

'Dynamite.'

'Good. See you Monday.'

He went back to the book he had been reading, and I went back to the Piccadilly. I explained what had happened to the wardrobe mistress and offered to find a replacement by Monday.

'Oh, don't worry, dear. I'll find somebody. You go and enjoy it. I've heard it's exciting.'

It was as simple as that. Exciting it was, and lots more.

Dennis – that was his name – was as good as his word. He hadn't warned me about the intense heat in the lime box, which he didn't seem to notice, but luckily for me on that first Monday night I only had a T-shirt on under my flying jacket. It was like a furnace in the box when all the arcs were blazing. It was the one time I was glad to have come from a line of stokers.

For the uninitiated, the terrific white light of the carbon arc, or follow spot as it's known to performers, which is projected from the farthest point in the auditorium over the heads of the audience on to the stage and is still the brightest in the theatre, is a live beam produced by fusing two carbon rods together and passing electricity through them. By means of mirrors this giant spark is reflected through a tunnel within the lamp and thrown out via the lamp's mouth. A good deal of care and attention is needed to maintain the two carbons, which are wound on manually from the side of the lamp, at the angle and distance which will give the optimum effect.

The show-plan for my lamp was a series of pencilled numbers drawn on the whitewashed wall above my section of the window at the front of the lime box. Attached to the top of my lamp was a piece of wire with a circle twisted into it. I had to line up this circle with a number on the wall, like a viewfinder in a camera. When I heard the number and 'get ready' cue over the Tannoy from the prompt corner, I fired up my lamp by bringing the carbons together, making sure that the front shutters, or eyelids, were closed. When the 'go' cue came I opened the shutters and with the spotlight picked up my artist whom I 'followed' until the end of the number.

Those are the basics, and that was all I knew for that first show. None of it could have prepared me for what actually happened when the curtain went up. The power that came out of the pit and across the footlights was stunning. I sometimes think that the hundreds of verbal cues whispered over our receiver and going out to Tannoys all over the theatre even added to the excitement. I've listened to public and critics alike commenting on the greatness of various musicals but I saw the original London version of *West Side*

Story over a hundred times and every night it took my breath away.

Perched on my high stool in the lime box at Her Majesty's, I witnessed a standard of theatrical excellence that I had never before encountered. I experienced the sheer elation of being party to the creation of something perfect. During the curtain calls I would often skip out of the theatre to watch the audience streaming through the foyer and on to the street, the glow still on their faces. I became a living ad. for the show – persuading friends and acquaintances to go, saving up to buy tickets for my family – in an attempt to get everyone I knew in while it lasted. I had the feeling that it would be a long time before London saw the likes of this again.

Suddenly, after years of being bored at school, never able to concentrate properly on anything, dreaming my life away, I could hardly wait to get out of bed in the morning. I was anxious to soak up anything I could, and once Dennis realised this he would lend me to other backstage departments. Another would-be artiste, Ros Drinkwater, with those Bluebell legs, had joined us in the lime box, so, with Jo, the chief spark's wife, we were four. With Ros in attendance, Dennis and Jo were quite capable of carrying the whole show on the limes, while I gradually picked up professional experience in all the other departments.

I had lots of fantasies about the girls in the show, but I didn't come into contact with any of them until I started working at stage level. Roberta Keith, who played one of the girl Sharks, touched me where I was most vulnerable. One night she saw me eyeing the trays of uneaten food which the management was required to provide for US Equity members between shows every Wednesday and Saturday. She invited me up to the dressing-room which she shared with Gloria, a coffee-coloured B.B. from Harlem, and laid half a dozen burgers on me. After that I became very popular with my flatmates, in much the same way as Dad had been when he'd brought food home from his first full-time job. Meanwhile, Roberta became popular with me. I introduced Baxter to Gloria and we went out on some wonderful double dates.

Gradually, through my friendship with the girls, I met everybody in the cast. They were a modest and unsnobby lot. When they heard that I was a drama student studying Shakespeare and the classics, you'd have thought I was in the hit show and they were working the lights. In those Americans I discovered a dedication to work that I'd never before encountered. For some it was their début show, which I found hard to believe. George Chakiris told me that it was the first time he had danced on stage; he had picked up the routines during rehearsal.

I was particularly inspired by a young actor who was just starting out by playing the goofy Master of Ceremonies in the dance-hall scene. During the run of the show, as the original cast started to drift back to the United States, he rose through the ranks, first taking over the role of Doc from an actor thirty years his senior, and eventually replacing Don McKay as Tony, the Romeo and main character of the musical. His name was David Holliday and he became a firm chum who taught me more about guts than he ever could have guessed. He finally left *West Side Story* to star with Elaine Stritch in Noël Coward's musical *Sail Away* at the Savoy.

Things really started looking up in my second term at Webber D. I no longer felt so alien and was even able to share in the excitement of the castings of the much talked-about *Othello*. It was announced that I would play Iago and Stuart Hoyle would play Othello, but things did not turn out quite as we'd planned that day outside Dino's. We learned that the production would be divided into two wholly separate casts, one of which would perform the first two acts, and the other would play through to the end. In the first half Brian Coburn would be the Moor and I would play Iago. Stuart Hoyle would then take over the title role in the second half, playing with Peter Smith. Stuart and I wouldn't play together at all. Our only correct assumption was that Peter Bucknell would direct.

During the first term I hadn't come to grips with voice lessons. To all the other classes – mime, movement, make-up, fencing, improvisation – I'd taken like a cat to tuna. But the twice-weekly voice lessons, one for elocution and one for voice production, just weren't working out. Somehow I couldn't summon up the required level of enthusiasm and it always seemed to me that there was so much else to do. I reassured myself with the thought that I had a natural ear and could pick up accents like a parrot. Rather than speaking 'proper', I would treat standard English roles as a dialect.

Iago put the stopper on that idea. At the first speech class of the new term Kathleen Fleming introduced herself. She was in her thirties and she had the most beautiful voice I'd ever heard. I was content just to be in her class and have that lovely voice wash over me until, one day, my verbal thrust and parries having failed to deter her, she got on my case.

I had just given a particularly inept rendition of a John Donne sonnet for the benefit of the class. When I finished, there was a pause, and then she recited the entire thing from memory. I can't imagine that she spoke it in one breath, but that was the impression she gave. It was such an evenly paced, seamless performance that I felt I had to talk to her about it so I hung behind after the others had gone. It was the last class of the day so she invited me to walk with her to the Underground. She said that, although I wasn't aware of it, and might not believe it, I had a strong, original voice.

'I can't give you a voice if you haven't already got one, but if it is there I can help you free it. That's my job; that's what I do. I understand your problems.'

I laughed self-consciously. I felt like the Beast listening to Beauty.

She went on, 'Don't laugh. I do. I've been there myself. You can do it and I can help you but you have to trust me and you have to work.'

We had reached Gloucester Road Station and she was making for the District Line entrance.

I asked which way she was going.

'East,' she replied, so I thought I would tag along as far as Charing Cross.

I always liked the District Line platform at Gloucester Road, liked the way the trains came up out of the tunnel for air. While we waited, Kathleen talked a little about breathing. I didn't breathe properly, she said. When our train arrived, she was still talking animatedly, and by the time we'd pulled in to Charing Cross I'd decided that there was no reason why I had to go home before reporting for work at the theatre.

The train entered familiar territory: Bethnal Green, Mile End, Bow Road.

'Where do you get off?' I asked.

'A few stations from now: Plaistow.'

'Plaistow?' I said. *'Plaistow?'*

'Plaistow,' she said, pronouncing it correctly.

'Whereabouts in Plaistow?'

'Shipman Road; Twenty-one Shipman Road.'

'Not Shipman Road, past the library?'

'Past the library. Yes.'

'I can't believe it.'

'We are going to have to do something about that "a", Terence,' she said.

When the train pulled in to Plaistow we strolled along the platform and up the stairs towards the exit. I told her, 'Me mum and dad still live in Chadwin Road.'

We said goodbye at the ticket collector's gate. As I turned to go back down the stairs to the westbound platform, Kate Fleming called out, 'I told you I understood your problems.'

Every Sunday from then on, after I'd scoffed Mum's roast lunch, I'd walk over to Shipman Road where Kate's mother would give me tea and then we'd set to work 'freeing my voice'. These were my first 'private lessons'. Whenever I had a quid to spare I gave it to Kate, but her normal fee was never discussed.

As I was preparing to play Iago, we used the text for a lot of our sessions together. Kate revealed some of her insights into Iago. Being something of an introvert, she gave a completely different reading of the piece from that which Bucknell the extrovert was urging on me at rehearsals. Later in Kate Fleming's career she was discovered by Laurence Olivier. In my opinion, it was with her help that he achieved in his Othello a vocal compass and breadth which surprised even his most devoted followers.

My life was taken over by the obsessed Iago. I told myself that if I could pull this off it wouldn't really matter if nobody saw my performance. I'd have done it, and everything thereafter would be a doddle. There would never be a villain I couldn't reach or get hold of.

Kate used to talk about the essential core of a character. She was a great one for going straight to the heart and letting the rest fall into place.

'It can be frightening,' she warned. 'Yes, Iago's a fictitious character but, once you've located similar traits in yourself, all you have to do is bring them out. And *that* is the big own up! It's like confessing in public: I have that. It's part of me. Part of my make-up. That's where actors start to lie. They're not even aware of it, but there's that bit that hangs on, that says, "I'm just the actor. I'm nice really, I'm not like him." Iago can't let that happen. It would be like playing with a sheet of perspex separating you from the audience. Iago is the ultimate threat, the arrow into the unknown, that place where nobody in the audience wants to look. Iago says, "I'm it, you can't kid me." '

One Sunday evening, while walking back to Chadwin Road to say goodbye to my folks, I was reflecting on Kate's penetrating insights when a thought occurred to me. If I were really Iago, what would I be like? How would I actually be seeing the world as I walked past the Prince Regent's Lane library? Well, for a start, I wouldn't be at peace, with anything or anybody. I'd be squirming with envy and discontent, seeing the worst in everyone, expecting the worst, lashing out. I decided to give it a try.

Wrapping myself in Iago's negativity, I walked into the park. It was a route I'd taken since childhood, a path between the lido and the disused playground. I tried to see the worst in everything. Familiar landmarks took on a different and menacing appearance. Even looking at courting couples, my thoughts became: Maim him! Rape her! The pushed-through knot-holes in the planked lido fence became ominous whereas before they'd been a useful device for watching swimmers.

I shifted my attention to the abandoned playground which had been derelict since we first moved to Chadwin Road. I knew and loved the rusted ribs of the umbrella roundabout, the abused remains of the triple-horse seesaw, its wooden skirt and horsehead handles long since gone, and the single hanging bar. Nobody had ever questioned why the playground at this end of the park – our end – had been allowed to fall into such disrepair. We liked it just as it was. It was exclusive to us. As I took everything in, I remembered the first spectre of an orgasm I'd experienced on that long-suffering hanging bar. Taller mates could jump up, grab it and hand over hand the length of it. I could only just touch it, let alone hold on. On trips to the library to return Ethel's often overdue books, I would stop at the playground and try in vain to join that élite club along with my peers Johnny Straffon and Georgie Smith. I must have been ten or eleven when one day I placed Ethel's books on the tarmac and, using them as a step, managed a few hand-overs with a lot of wriggling and heavy breathing, my shirt coming adrift. I was about halfway across, when I ran out of strength. I'd never made it this far before so, in true crablike fashion, I hung on, trying to amass new energy, but at the same time realising that the longer I waited the more tired my arms would become. I tensed for one last swing before I dropped down. As I did so a wonderful sensation warmed my body. I was so intent on completing my task that by the time my brain focused on the feeling it had already begun to fade. I had no inkling that this sensation was sexual. If I had I might have spent my life seeking increasingly stressful parallel bars.

And Iago? What if he had experienced his first orgasmic sensation during an act of malevolence? What roads would *he* then tread in order to secure a reoccurrence? In that moment I felt that I had grasped the mettle of his psyche. I had found my star motivation, as Stanislavski termed it.

Nine
Blacker Than Othello

Peter Bucknell was a modern, volatile and inspiring director. From the first day of rehearsal, when he leapt into the theatre like a flame, with his red sweater and his college-boy haircut, I felt that I could trust him to pick me up, carry me somewhere and put me safely down again. It was a feeling not unlike the commitment you feel in a cinema after seeing the opening frames, when you know that you can trust the director not to drop you midway.

Bucknell didn't let us down, any of us. Twelve weeks may sound ample time to devote to rehearsals for a play, or, to be accurate, half a play, but at the time it seemed to me that I could have used twice as long. I was also playing Mr Hardcastle in *Love on the Dole*, again directed by Helen Lowry.

Working on flatmate George's principle of knowing the words first and last, I decided to learn my lines for Iago straight away. I promised myself that I would master five pages daily. As the part of Iago was longer than anything I'd ever done before, I was by no means certain that I'd remember it all. Every morning, as soon as I awoke, I would face into a corner, close my eyes and run through the lines I'd learnt the day before as if they were one speech. If I'd forgotten anything, I relearned the lines before starting the quota for that day. What a burden is lifted once the words are committed to memory. Most of my fears about acting are fuelled by the possibility of not being able to master my lines. I understood this from the moment I began in *Othello*. Since then I've always tried to put any other worries aside until I've learned the words. I invariably see things in a different light once I've done so.

One day I'd been fortunate enough to come upon Wilfred Lawson on the Metropolitan Line. There he was, sitting opposite me, his shoes gleaming like a guardsman's boots, greeting his fellow travellers with a lopsided grin. I couldn't believe my luck.

Lawson was one of the greatest actors who ever drew breath. For a while I sat transfixed, watching as he took a casual morning look at his universe. Eventually, fearing that he might suddenly alight from the train, I seized the moment and found the courage to say, 'I'm an actor, just starting. Is there any advice . . . you could give me?'

'Advice.' The voice – I'd heard it so many times from the anonymity of an audience – chuckled the word back at me as if speaking it for the very first time.

'Yes.' I gained courage from his obvious sympathy. 'What do *you* do?'

His eyes rolled, as though scanning an inner dimension where words didn't exist. A cherubic smile moved on his lips.

I waited for the great man to speak.

'Oh, I just learn the wordies,' he finally said.

This succinct advice proved to be invaluable.

There is often a moment when the brain can't or won't take any more in. I think it's possible to get stuck at that point and to become convinced that this failure is a permanent condition. Some film actors don't bother to learn their lines at all. I once observed Brando struggling to memorise the first line of a speech he had written on cue cards during the filming of *Superman*. I asked him how he would ever play Macbeth and Lear if he couldn't learn this stuff.

He didn't pause for a second. 'I've learnt *them* already,' he said.

Rehearsals for *Othello* were going along at a rate of knots. Brian Coburn was getting his bulk into the first half of Othello and Kenneth McReddie, who was playing Roderigo, showed an early grasp of his character. Ken and I had to open the piece and Bucknell spent a lot of time making sure we had the right pace.

Stuart Hoyle never raised the subject of Mike Jackson's agent friend again. Whenever I mentioned it his response was cool, as though he wished he'd never spoken to me about it in the first place. I began to feel his eyes on me during rehearsals. Although we were treated as two separate casts, Bucknell encouraged everyone to be present at rehearsals for both halves of the play. I wondered vaguely whether Stuart was waiting to see how I would shape up but I couldn't pin this feeling on to anything in particular. I waited for him to give me his views about what I was doing or perhaps a note or two. He didn't. We never had coffee together unless I suggested it.

Eventually I thought, Right, I've got to nail this down, so I invited him to Dino's. He seemed his usual easy-going self and talked a lot about a girl named Eva Wishaw in the year above. I had noticed her myself. She had that fair, cool skin which is sometimes found in English girls. She also had terrific legs. Making certain that I wasn't in Iago-vision, I asked him if he'd heard anything from Mike about his agent chum. Stuart switched off and tried to change the subject. Not willing to be put off, I said that perhaps Mike Jackson wasn't too friendly with this agent, after all. Perhaps he didn't even know any agent. And it was strange that Anthony Newley hadn't shown up at the Christmas do.

Stuart jumped to his chum's defence. Apparently, he'd heard Mike talking to Jimmy Fraser at his office on several occasions.

'Jimmy Fraser? Is that the agent?'

He nodded, sorry he'd let the name out.

'What's the problem then, Stu? Is he going to invite him or not?'

Stuart huffed and puffed a bit. 'He's just waiting to see if this production is good enough – or the right one, that's all.'

I let the matter drop. We went back to lecherous observations about the lovely Eva. But I had a hunch that something was wrong and I took the matter to George.

'Jimmy Fraser. Is that who is coming?' he wanted to know.

'I'm not sure yet; Stuart keeps stalling.'

'I understand, but is that the agent?'

'Yes. That's what he said: Jimmy Fraser. D'you know him?'

'I wish I did.'

'Is he good, then?'

'Well, you know there's the big agents – English agents swallowed up by American outfits – and then there's the independents. I'd say Fraser and Dunlop is the best of those – in the top three, anyway.'

'What's his problem, then? If his mate couldn't raise the guy, why doesn't he just say so? He was so keen last term. He put the idea into my head in the first place.'

'Different now, though, isn't it? Sounds like he's got to give his friend the go-ahead. Sounds like you're a bit too good; might steal his thunder.'

'But we're so different,' I said. 'There's no conflict, really.'

'He won't see it like that. You know what actors are.' George grinned the familiar grin, his face creasing like linen. 'All's fair in love and showbiz.'

All evening I turned over in my mind everything that George had said. It was now the middle of February. There was roughly one month before the show, before the one and only performance we would give.

I decided to approach the situation as Iago would have done. I wanted the chance. If this agent, Mr Fraser, came to the *Othello* performance to see Stuart, he would also see me. I had to convince Stuart that I was not a threat. I decided to act deliberately badly for the remaining four weeks of rehearsal. If I was wrong, and it was just my paranoia, that was fine. But, if I was right, it would be a worthwhile gamble.

As the quality of my performance deteriorated, Peter Bucknell raised an eyebrow or two and I began to get lots of notes. But I quite enjoyed taking on my new persona. I felt like a pool hustler; I felt like Iago. At each rehearsal I did one section as I hoped to play it on the night. Over the four weeks I was thus able to try out most of my ideas and feel sure that the character was developing solidly. On Saturday mornings I would get up early, do my exercises and walk up to Regent's Park. I'd find a deserted spot and try my soliloquies in the open air, really letting rip.

David Holliday, my chum from *West Side Story*, had become a great fan of the London theatre scene. He'd attended matinée performances of all West End plays that didn't clash with *West Side Story*. His favourite was Michael Elliot's production of Ibsen's *Brand* at the Lyric, Hammersmith, with Patrick McGoohan. Holliday saw it as many times as he could. As our performance of *Othello* approached, he asked whether I could sneak him in to see some of the rehearsals. I was delighted, and I took him round to Bucknell's studio in Clareville Grove. I introduced Holliday, and asked Bucknell whether my friend could watch one of our rehearsals. I think Peter Bucknell was flattered. Anybody from the cast of *West Side Story* was a hero. He invited David to come to an afternoon dress rehearsal the following day.

Since the start of rehearsals I'd visualised Iago with a shaped beard, but, when I'd stopped shaving to see how it would look, my beard grew so patchily that I'd abandoned the idea. On the morning of the dress rehearsal, Peter Bucknell suggested that I might try to draw on a beard, or make one. I decided to experiment with a combination of the two. I used my black Leichner stick to etch the basic shape and stuck a few tufts of hair on the point of my chin to give it added dimension.

At three o'clock David Holliday was out front with Bucknell. Everybody in the cast was nervous and excited. At the last minute Richard Davies, who was playing Cassio, told me how to keep my tights from drooping by twisting halfpennies into the tops and then using them like buttons to brace them up. The boys' dressing-room was so cramped that the second team couldn't come in until we'd left. As I was going down for curtain-up, Stuart passed me on the stairs, wished me luck and casually mentioned to me that the agent, Jimmy Fraser, would be in the following night for the main event. This news didn't alter my plan, but I was thrilled to bits. As I hadn't yet had a chance to go properly through the role, I decided to give it my all for this run-through. I would tone it down the following day if it seemed too over the top. Afterwards, I knew there were moments when my performance had got out of hand, but most of it was fine. Peter Bucknell gave us notes after we'd finished our half of the play. He told me to tighten up a few things, but basically he gave me a thumbs-up.

Those of us in the first half had the luxury of being able to watch the second half from the stalls. I sat at the back to see how it sounded. One thing I noticed was that Peter Smith, who played the second half of Iago, looked in only one direction when doing his soliloquies. As I watched him I hit upon the idea of including as much of the audience as I could with my glances in order to maximise the effect. Kate Fleming had said Iago was the arrow shot at the spectators and I didn't want to limit my target. It is, after all, in Iago's soliloquies that he bares his darkest secrets.

Just before the end of the show David Holliday had to leave to do his obligatory warm-up at Her Majesty's. He gestured to me to indicate that we'd chat later.

I went to Her Majesty's that night to explain to a stand-in my cues for the two shows I would miss the next day. David had already spread the word, and many of the *West Side Story* cast congratulated me and wished me well when I arrived. When the final curtain came down, he was waiting for me at the stage door and took me out to The Pier, a little restaurant he knew I liked in Marylebone Road. We talked about my performance and he made a few suggestions for improvements. One of the things he particularly liked was the frenzy that came over me whenever I was left alone on stage, as though I was just bursting to tell the audience what villainies I was up to. He left me in a very positive frame of mind, and, as I lay in bed that night, my mind kept returning to another special night.

In the Fifties, a charity show called 'The Night of a Hundred Stars' was put on every year at the London Palladium. As a boy I'd heard of this sumptuous gala and always had a yen to be there. Two gentlemen, who were wealthy, retired and living in Switzerland, spent the entire year making the preparations for this one glittering evening. The gala started at midnight so that working performers could take part. The proceeds went to an actors' charity and, as the biggest names were happy to appear, ticket prices were phenomenal.

This year's show had been no exception. I'd heard that George Chakiris and Elizabeth Seal had been asked to dance a number called 'Steam Heat' from *Pajama Game*. One evening I bumped into George in the Haymarket on our way to Her Majesty's. He said he'd been rehearsing for the big gala.

'Is it going OK?' I asked.

'I'm petrified I'm going to drop the hat,' said Chakiris. He already looked petrified.

'That's one evening I'd love to be part of, George,' I said.

'It's good, is it?'

'Yeah.'

'Tickets a lot of bread?' he asked.

'Oh yeah. Some seats cost hundreds, but if I could tag along with you – as your dresser, say – I could watch it from the wings.'

'Sure, I'll take you in. We'll meet after the show Saturday night.'

I could hardly wait for the weekend to arrive.

Saturday came. I watched George dance both shows – matinée and evening – from the lime box, and then I waited for him at the stage door. After a quick snack at the Egg and I in the Haymarket, we took a cab to the stage door of the Palladium. A pack of autograph hunters were waiting outside the back gate near the stage door and George signed a few books.

'Evening, I'm George Chakiris,' he said to the stage doorman. 'This is Terence; he's with me.'

'Evening, Sir. Your dressing-room's round to the left; your name's on the door.'

We were in. When we reached the dressing-room, George turned to me and said, 'OK?'

'Thanks, George. Listen, is there anything you want? I'm here to give you a hand.'

'No. You push off and have a good time.' Then he rubbed his throat. 'Say, you haven't got a lifesaver, by any chance?'

'What?'

'I'm so dry – a lifesaver, a candy.'

'Wait here. I'll find you one.'

I nipped through a few passages. A loudspeaker was announcing overture and beginners. Everybody around me was fraught. It was hardly the moment to stop someone and ask whether they had a boiled sweet. I made my way back to the stage door. I said to the doorman, 'I've got to get something for Mr Chakiris. You'll know me when I come back?'

'I'll know you, son. If they stop you at the front there,' he pointed down the alley towards Great Marlborough Street, 'you tell them Bert said to let you in.'

Outside the gate I turned right and headed towards Argyll Street and the main entrance of the theatre. There was a kiosk just past the front doors, but it was closed. I hurried back to the steps of the Palladium where latecomers were still scurrying up the stairs. They'd all made an effort and were done up like dogs' dinners.

One man, a dashing figure in evening dress, stood out among the rest. He was selling programmes but, in their hurry not to miss the overture, people were rushing by oblivious to him.

I heard him crying, 'Programme. Anybody want a programme? Gimme a pound for a programme.'

I'd have known that voice anywhere. I took a few steps to get a closer look.

It was Cary Grant.

He smiled at me and said, 'Wanna programme? Cost yer ten bob. Last-minute reduction.'

I said, 'I'd love a programme but I haven't got two pennies to rub together.' Suddenly he was off, wares under his arm. I watched those long, agile legs taking the stairs two at a time. I kicked myself. I had been face to face with my all-time idol, and had only managed a glimpse of the famous dimple.

I was getting desperate. I spied a kindly face at a ticket window. The words tumbled out of me.

'You haven't got a boiled sweet, have you? I've this mate in the show. He's doing "Steam Heat", and he's a bit dry in the throat.'

The woman behind the glass smiled, but before she could answer a voice behind me asked, 'What's his name, your mate?'

'George,' I said, 'George Chakiris.'

'Here, help yourself.'

I turned. A blond gent with watered silk lapels and matching bow tie was holding a bag of sweets towards me. Fox's Glacier Mints.

'I hope he doesn't drop the hat,' he said.

I grabbed a fistful. 'He won't,' I yelled over my shoulder.

The final bars of the overture could be heard as I slipped into the wings, trying not to be noticed. The familiar aroma of size intermingled with the expensive perfumes which floated across the footlights when the curtain was whisked away. A hush descended and then the audience and artists became one.

My first and only night of a hundred stars.

George didn't drop the hat.

Funny, the events which shape your life. Sometimes you scarcely notice them, never realising their importance at the time.

On the morning of the great day I woke up and did some exercises, really working my feet and stomach. I then made myself a mug of tea. I have never liked tea made with tea-bags, but, before the tea manufacturers convinced the working class that it was smart, I was in the habit of brewing a single mug of tea by filling a strainer with a spoonful of loose leaves and then leaving it to steep for a few minutes. On this particular Saturday morning I took my mug into the bathroom with me. By nine-thirty I had finished a leisurely bath, shaved and washed my hair. I planned to be at the Chanticleer Theatre by six o'clock, which would allow me an hour and a half to experiment with the beard and get into costume before curtain-up at seven-thirty.

The whole day lay before me. I decided to pay my mum a visit. As soon as it occurred to me, I knew it was exactly what I wanted to do. I strolled to Oxford Street. The first number 15 which went past was too full, but I jumped on to the second: destination EASTHAM – THE WHITE HORSE, location of my first sighting of a woman in an ankle bracelet.

I commandeered my favourite seat – left-hand front lower deck – which offered an uninterrupted panoramic view. (Nowadays this lordly viewpoint is often deliberately obscured by London Transport's posters threatening punishment for graffiti.) How admirable are our London buses! Who would willingly replace this envy of the civilised world with the closed-in driver-only monstrosity?

With my brain in neutral, after weeks of effort, I took in the sights as we cruised down Regent Street: past the fur shop I promised to take my mother to when my ship came in; past the old Hamley's toy shop where I'd stood for hours one Christmas watching a man making balloons from a tube; past the Café Royal whose doors I hadn't yet stepped through but would one day with the girl of my dreams.

As the bus chugged east, its throbbing power connected to my right foot and the string of landmarks brought back memories of my childhood.

The grand red Route Master finally delivered me to the Greengate. I bought a packet of Senior Service in the tobacconist on the corner and took a leak in the below-ground public conveniences opposite, the splendid urinal still proudly displaying its single bee trademark in spite of countless dousings. It was only eleven o'clock. I strolled along to my Uncle Harry's favourite shop: the Book

113

Exchange and Mart. As a child I had smelled the ancient books and idled among old companions such as Peter Cheyney, Leslie Charteris, Hank Janson. The shop was smaller than I remembered it; that must be a sure sign of growing up. Strolling along Barking Road, I looked in to say hello to Ambrose, the barber's where as a boy I used to have my hair cut on a Saturday. The smell of shaving soap and bay rum wafted at me as I entered. It made me think of the mates I'd abandoned when I left the East End. I kept thinking about David Taylor and his mother Florrie. I'd practically lived in their grand house in Cumberland Road, with its lush carpets and cut-glass bowls filled with fruit. Our Saturday nights at the Magenta or Lotus Ballrooms. We'd had to dream up schemes to chat up girls because we couldn't dance. I missed it all. I knew I had to make my mark before I could spend time in Plaistow and risk being drawn back into its cosy existence.

My dad was at work, but Mum was in. Six-month-old John was slumbering in his pram near the fireplace in the living-room.

'Have you time for something to eat?' Mum wanted to know.

'Don't go to a lot of trouble; a fried-egg sandwich'll be fine.'

'I'll do you an egg and chips. It's no trouble. It'll only take a minute.'

My leaving home had made no difference to Mum's regime: she still lovingly prepared three meals a day.

I fill the kettle from the brass tap at the sink and put it on to the gas. We quickly slip into our old routine, but Mum is oblivious of my impending ordeal. She can't help me because I haven't told her. Mum is ignorant of the fact that my life may change. This evening, for Christ's sake.

Soon the small scullery is filled with the sizzling sound of hot fat and potato juice. I sit on the step leading into the kitchen, my legs stretched out in front of me. I watch my mother at the stove, her midriff still thick from the recent addition to the family: her sixth child, counting the miscarriage. How youthful she looks. The arms are chubby, but still like a young girl's. I remember the time when Lynette was born at home and the arctic zone of the front room was unexpectedly filled with warmth. It was Christmas: 23 December 1951. Lynette Mary was an extra present for Mum: her long-awaited daughter. What goes on inside women? What turmoil does pregnancy create? They certainly look wonderful when all the hormones swing into overdrive.

For once the empathy with my mother that I'd come to depend upon wasn't there. I had to remind myself that she had no knowledge of my West End life or the confusion it was causing within me. I wanted to have my cake and eat it as well.

The egg and chips were classic. They always were. I had a couple of cups of tea, the kind you only get at home, and I flipped through *Woman's Own* to see if Gypsy Petulengro foresaw anything in my stars.

I started to feel agitated and I went out into the yard. Dad's corrugated-iron shed, the Ponderosa, was getting rusty. I was about to make a move when I felt pressure on my bladder. The tea had run straight through me. My body knew I was nervous even though my brain was not computing it. Resisting the impulse to run through my lines, I lifted the latch on the door of our outside loo and stepped inside. As I relieved myself I started to think about the hours I must have spent in that draughty closet. I buttoned up my fly, lowered the scrubbed wooden seat and sat down. There was a San Izal loo roll – curiously non-absorbent, akin to greaseproof paper – hanging like a necklace on its own loop of string from a nail in the wall. That same nail had accompanied many boyhood reflections when I had sought the privacy of the outside loo. In those days squares of neatly torn newsprint had been pushed on to the nail one at a time like important memos. I looked around for other improvements. Now the walls were distempered green. The bizarre coating hadn't contained the rising damp on the outside walls and bubbles festered like scoops of pistachio ice-cream.

It was the flush release that triggered a kind of shame within me. Here, more than anywhere, was evidence of my folks' efforts to maintain appearances and to keep abreast of their upwardly moving neighbours. The pink and white rubber pendant was also hanging by string – a shadow of its chrome-linked self – tied to the metal elbow of the cistern up above. I could imagine Ethel's eye being caught by this bauble, unaware of the new built-in obsolescence which accompanied the war-time breakthrough in technology.

I was ashamed not for Mum and Dad, but for myself. How little I had contributed. So few of my efforts had been to make life better and more interesting for them. Tears came to my eyes, but I was suddenly aware of another, stronger feeling: a solid resolve to make something of myself. I left the only remaining outside loo on the street with a spring in my step.

Ten

Paradise in Piccadilly

Samantha Eggar, or Sam as she was affectionately called by her friends, had definitely caught my eye. My interest was unrequited, of course; a condition as necessary to the romantically inclined as bitter chocolate to a mousse. But I could no longer ignore the fact that I was more than a little taken by her. There was an ingenuous quality about her which was devastating.

I didn't seek her out, but was always pleased to see her. She was filled to the brim with laughter during those first few terms. When I heard her chuckles rippling through the corridors of Webber D, I would feel perked up, regardless of the time of day. Sometimes she would leave the school just ahead of me, wearing an outrageously large suede jacket over her slight shoulders. I wondered how she'd come by that jacket. I would walk behind her as she made for the Piccadilly Line, her long slim legs taking almost pigeon-toed steps. She was much taken by all things American and wore a chain with US dog tags around her neck. She lit her cigarettes with a genuine Zippo lighter, confidently finger-snapping it open and shut. She wore jeans even in winter. Old Spice aftershave was her cologne. An unusual scent at the time, its aroma lingered in the commonroom after she'd gone to class.

Occasionally her jade eyes would fix on mine for a second, then she would grin, baring head-girl teeth and gums. She knew that I was holding back; the fact seemed to amuse her. There were rumours that she still carried a torch for a distant cousin known as Dandy Kim whom she believed glamorous and whom she had endowed with all kinds of mysterious qualities. She often carried a book entitled *Chocolates for Breakfast* in which Dandy Kim was fictionalised. Rick Jones, in the same year as us, had also touched her heart and she held a soft spot for him. I was rarely alone with her and consoled myself with the thought that such a creature would have eyes for me one day. There were many

119

beautiful girls at Webber D, but Sam was a most serious distraction.

On that fateful Saturday, when I arrived at school to start my preparations for the performance, I found a little pile of cards and gifts awaiting me, apparently an old theatrical tradition. I looked at my good-luck mementoes but there was nothing from Sam. Next I opened my faithful cardboard make-up box and laid out my grease-paints. This time I didn't use a solid black base, but drew the basic shape on in grey, and then, as though plaiting raffia, built up layers of dark colours, finishing off with a few bright slashes of red, blue and purple. By the time I had stuck on a few tufts of crêpe hair the beard looked quirky but not bad. Near me Brian Coburn had been putting on his black face and we had a moment to compare our handiwork before the rest of the cast started trooping in. Ken McReddie looked startling in full make-up, like an El Greco.

I was busy thinking about the problem of my stage entrance when I caught the aroma of Old Spice. I looked up and saw the reflection of Samantha sidling through the door. She came up behind me, saying, 'Excuse me, boys. I only need a moment.'

She smiled her picnic smile into the mirror and put a pack of Camel on to my section of the dressing-room table. I had never seen her so dressed up.

'Where are you off to?' I asked.

'I'm going to see the play, dummy, so you'd better be good.' Then she put her hand on my shoulder and leaned over me. 'And . . . I'm loaning you this, for good luck.' She put her trusty Zippo on top of the packet of Camels. 'It has a piece of string tied to it. OK?' Then, with a fast 'Have a good show', she was gone, just her scent left hanging in the air. She had touched my shoulder; it was so light I could have missed it. But I didn't.

Peter Bucknell whisked by to wish us all the best and issued a last instruction to keep it tight. 'Remember: "Two hours' traffic on our stage." '

Stuart came in just as we had been called down to the wings. He gave me a hug and whispered, 'He's here.' Perhaps I had been wrong about Stuart, after all.

Sliding across the warm stage, Ken and I made our way to the OP side, trying not to hear the excited buzz beyond the curtain.

The confined space had that dusty, painted aroma of stages the world over. We looked at each other and smiled self-consciously. Ken looked young and vulnerable; hardly out of short trousers.

'All the best, Ken.'

'Yes, break a leg, T.'

The narrow gap between the side curtain and the outside wall of the theatre – the wing from where we were to make our entrance – could accommodate only one person, so Ken positioned himself downstage and I flattened myself against the wall next to him.

Somebody whispered across to us, 'Curtain going up in five seconds.' We heard the curtain being whisked away and then the taped chimes of the clock started to toll. On the last clock-strike we were on. I drew my left leg up behind me and placed my foot flat against the wall. I gave Ken a second to get clear of the drapes. He was saying, 'Tush, never tell me,' as I kicked myself on to stage.

In my wildest dreams I hadn't expected it to go so well. Peter Bucknell had directed us in a fast, tight production and nobody put a foot wrong. We didn't need to improvise or change anything. But within these edicts I found a new and unsuspected fervour. It just happened as I played my part, leaving me no space for extraneous thought or fear, tantamount to the same thing on stage. During my first soliloquy I felt a ripple of shock as the audience registered that I was actually talking to them not as a single, anonymous block sitting passively in their seats, but as individuals who were included in the action. When I went into the second soliloquy, I glanced out at the sea of faces as soon as the stage was clear, and paused as if to say, 'It's you and me again, folks.' I took up my position a foot away from the front edge of the stage, planting my feet squarely on the boards. Then, looking up into the back of the auditorium, I began my speech. I wasn't doing anything differently from the way we'd planned it in rehearsals, but as I started the delivery I felt myself growing, like Jack's beanstalk. My feet were rooted to the stage but my head and shoulders were going up, up, reaching the ceiling, taking in the whole auditorium. From then on, whenever I was alone onstage, this sensation took over.

It seemed only a matter of moments before the final curtain came down and both casts took their bows. The production had obviously been a success. Other students came into the dressing-room to congratulate us and everybody was extremely up. Mike Jackson came backstage and told me how much he'd enjoyed the play. He asked whether I would join him, Stuart and Jimmy Fraser for a drink in the pub. I had the notion that it was unprofessional to leave the theatre without first removing all traces of make-up and, as I wanted to create the right impression with this important agent, I took longer than usual to remove my schlap.

I walked down to the Hereford Arms on the corner of Clareville Street. It was a good five minutes before I realised that I was in the wrong pub. I panicked. The Denmark was at the far end of Clareville Grove. I hared over there, but I needn't have worried. In the private bar were Mike and his friend, a tall imposing man with a warm smile and a Scottish burr. Mike introduced us.

Mr Fraser said, 'My God, that's the sexiest Iago I've ever seen! Thank goodness he's not loose on the streets.'

We chatted a bit. Mr Fraser said that when I thought about leaving school I should give him a ring.

At the beginning of the next term, after the Easter break, Stuart and Eva Wishaw astonished everyone at Webber D by getting married and taking a little flat in Old Brompton Road. Then, as if a trend had been set, Rick Jones married Marina, another girl in Sam's class. Sam didn't take too kindly to that. I began to think I might stand a chance with her by default. In April Moray Watson arrived to direct us in *While the Sun Shines*, a war-time escapist comedy by Terence Rattigan. Moray was then starring in a successful West End play, and we were greatly privileged to have a working actor actually taking time out to push us into shape. To know and be directed by him was certainly a big plus in my life.

As we started to read *While the Sun Shines* I remembered that Mum and I had listened to it on the wireless soon after the War, and I thus had a special affection for the piece. I was cast as the Earl of Harpenden, a part which, with his gift for light comedy, I thought Moray would have played to perfection.

The action takes place in the Earl's chambers in Albany. Terence Rattigan had chosen this prestigious setting in London's Piccadilly because Albany – or 'Paradise in Piccadilly', as it was known – was an oasis for many young aristocrats. Originally the mansion had been the property of the Duke of York and Albany, but in 1801 the spendthrift Duke was forced to put his house on the market. The property was purchased by a shrewd business-man named Alexander Copland for the princely sum of £37,000. Copland converted the mansion into apartments and hired a famous architect of the day, Henry Holland, to design buildings that would run along each side of the spacious gardens behind the house in order to house extra tenants. Albany became the first custom-built block of flats in Britain.

As part of my preparation for playing the Earl of Harpenden, I thought it would be helpful to see the place where I was supposed to be living, so I took myself off to Piccadilly to pick up some atmosphere. I walked up and down the north side of that street for at least half an hour without locating Albany. I had a vague feeling that it was near the old In and Out Club at the Park Lane end but, eventually despairing of ever finding it, I decided to walk on to Her Majesty's. Suddenly there it was: just past the Royal Acad-emy, a stone's throw from the Circus. Shielded from the bustle of Piccadilly by an imposing courtyard, the original mansion could have leaned across and shaken hands with Hatchard's bookshop.

I skirted a neat square of cars which were parked in the middle of the forecourt and approached a giant of a doorman, who with his crested top hat seemed seven feet tall.

'Anything I can do for you, Sir?' he asked from the top of the stone steps leading to the mansion's blue front doors.

'Is this the Albany?'

'That's right, Sir, this is Albany,' he replied.

'I – er – only wanted to have a look.'

'Perfectly all right, Sir.'

I walked up the steps one at a time. As I neared the top I could see past the main doors into a high sombre hallway, about twenty yards long. At the end of the hall was something that made my heart beat faster. There, stretching out in front of me with a gentle upward slope, was the magical covered walkway I had espied from the opposite end when I was a delivery boy at Wilkes Bros & Greenwood. I finally had a name for my Shangri-la.

*

I appeared in three other plays that term but it was the Rattigan play directed by Moray which took most of my attention. Moray was a marvellous teacher. At one point I had to repeat the word 'oh' three times. I just couldn't make anything of it at all, but when I appealed to Moray for a solution he came up onstage and did for those 'ohs' what Marlon did for 'Charlie' in *On the Waterfront*. He gave me real insight into light-comedy timing. One night Moray invited a few of us to come and see him perform in Hugh and Margaret Williams's comedy, *The Grass is Greener*. What an unforgettable event that was. I decided that the magic lay in the timing. Afterwards he took us all out to supper at the Seven Stars Restaurant on the first floor of the Lyon's Corner House in Coventry Street. It was the most splendid place I'd ever been to and it gave me my first glimpse into that night world where I imagined movie stars shone after dark.

There were a lot of firsts that evening. For one thing, the jacket potato didn't come with marge and vinegar but with sour cream and chives. The salad had tiny squares of hard-boiled egg sprinkled on it and a proper French dressing served separately. (At home we'd only ever had salad with vinegar, each ingredient marooned on its own plate.) I wasn't quite sure what I was eating but it tasted just fine and I understood how the English must have felt when spices first arrived from the East.

I'm sure Moray wasn't unaware of the effect the occasion was having on us. He was relaxed and witty, treating us as equals, and unobtrusively helping us out if we floundered. He asked me what I was going to do during the long summer break. I had just finished a fresh fruit salad and was lounging on the padded red leather banquette waiting for the black coffee that Moray had ordered with 'cream separate'. When, by way of reply, I mumbled something about finding it hard to make ends meet and having to get a temporary job, Moray said that I should accustom myself to the idea of being an actor and look for acting jobs. It was a timely reminder that the reason I'd left home and given up my cushy job in advertising was to become an actor. It set me thinking.

Coming out of school a few days later, I was caught in a heavy shower and took shelter in the doorway of the Chanticleer Theatre. While I was waiting Moray came by with a brolly and we walked to the Underground together. I asked him why he'd chosen to teach at Webber D. He explained that he had arrived in the West End after three years of repertory in the provinces where most days had been eighteen hours long and action-packed. As he now didn't have to report to the theatre until seven-thirty each evening, he had energy to burn. Five years earlier, at drama school, he'd benefited from working with professional actors and he wanted to pass this opportunity on. Although Webber D was considered a poor relation at that time, its students received a comprehensive grounding, including a course on stage management, which Moray knew from experience to be invaluable when starting in repertory.

'Did you think any more about trying for jobs in the hols?' he asked.

'Yeah, I have, but I don't know how to go about it.'

'Would you like me to drop a line to a few casting people? I know it's frowned on by Rossiter, but,' his pause more than conveyed what a tough world it was out there, 'I don't mind.'

'Well, if you could that would be great . . . '

'Now, what are you in at the moment?'

'I'm doing *Waters of the Moon* with Miriam Brickman and *Fresh Fields* with Adam O'Riordan.'

'What do you think?' Moray said.

'I'd prefer it if they saw me in *While the Sun Shines*.'

'Well, hold on, Terence. Your accent is still quite rough. You are meant to be playing an earl, you know.' He smiled to soften the blow. 'D'you think you can pull it together? We don't have long.'

'I'll try. It's just that I get along best with you; I don't relate much to the others. If you're OK with it, that's the best for me.'

Moray considered. 'Look, I should ask the others in the cast if it is all right with them to invite casting people. That's only fair.'

'Yes, that's fair.'

'I'm not sure they'll agree, but I'll – '

'Are you kidding? They'll agree all right.'

He asked them, and I was right about the reaction of the other members of the cast. Moray dashed off notes straight away to four people, but casting directors were evidently highly in demand. As the last week of rehearsal arrived, Moray told me that two of them weren't free for the evening of our show, one had said she'd try and one hadn't replied at all. George had said it was like getting blood out of a stone, even when you were in a play. I began to think that it must have been a minor miracle that James Fraser had shown up for _Othello_.

On the afternoon of the show Moray gave me a José Florez cigar box to put my make-up in. He'd signed it: 'To Terry – Success MW'. That day we received a lot of laughs from school kids who came to the show.

Afterwards Moray handed me a letter from Liz Evette, a casting director. She apologised for not making it to the performance but, as Moray had recommended me so highly, she suggested that I come in and see her. The letter was on Associated Rediffusion notepaper.

Moray winked. 'I'd give her a ring.'

'What do I say?'

'Oh, you'll think of something. Play it by ear; I always do.' Then he laughed. 'I've got an interview next week – I'm a bit nervous myself.'

'What is it for?'

'Stanley Donen and Cary Grant have bought the rights to _The Grass is Greener_. They were in to see it the other night and want to talk to me about doing the movie.' He was clearly excited. 'Cary is going to play Hugh's part, Deborah Kerr will be the wife, Bob Mitchum will be the American and Jean Simmons the friend.'

It was my turn to be excited. What a cast! 'That's wonderful, Moray, wonderful,' I said.

'If I get it.'

'Oh, come on, man. If they've been to see you in it, and they want to talk to you, that's it.' I was certain.

He smiled. 'I'm glad you're so confident. Anyway, call Liz. I'll let you know how I get on.'

I made the call, and a few days later I was on my way to 235 Regent Street. Moray may have thought I was confident but I certainly didn't feel it. Since leaving home I'd bought hardly any gear and was feeling the pinch where my wardrobe was concerned. I had the perfect outfit in mind: a sharp dark suit, black or navy blue; a cotton shirt with a cut-away collar and the top button loose; a tie, not flash, but knotted with a double Windsor; and a highly polished pair of black Oxfords. Not having any of the above items I was wearing my jeans and *Rebel Without a Cause* windcheater. My welted Saxones were almost down to the uppers and had gone the way of all my brown shoes: a last-ditch coating of oxblood polish to liven them up.

The fact was that I didn't feel up to this interview. I couldn't keep my mind on it at all. Walking to the appointment, I thought about how many times I had passed Verrey's restaurant, without a clue that the television station I was now heading for was right above. From time to time I would get moods when I imagined I was a speck of dust on a huge whirling globe. If possible, I would stay in bed when I felt like this, but on that day I was being shown into Liz Evette's first-floor office.

It wasn't like any office I'd come across before; it was more like a grand sitting-room. Miss Evette was at a desk and she invited me to sit on a sofa which faced long windows looking out on to Regent Street. There was a man with her whom she introduced as Monty Lyons. I was taken aback because he was wearing the outfit I'd visualised for myself, without the double Windsor. As soon as I sat down I realised that I was facing the window with my profile towards her. I wondered vaguely whether it was my bad side. I didn't know which was my bad side, but I was sure that I had been placed awkwardly to see how I'd cope.

I asked myself what Jimmy Dean would have done in the same situation. I twisted round to face the room and threw my left leg over the arm of the couch. Unfortunately, this exposed one of my clapped-out ankle socks: a powder-blue cotton number, with a top like a cake frill, all elastic ends up for air.

Miss Evette and Mr Lyons glanced at the culprit, and quickly turned their eyes away, but I caught the looks.

I squirmed and held my position. Dean would probably have picked up the ashtray, drawled into it, 'Have my driver bring the car round to the front,' and left the room.

I heard myself saying, 'Yes, I'm at the Webber Douglas.'

As Miss Evette's expression wasn't one of instant recognition and admiration, I added, 'Stewart Granger went there,' which also went down like a lead balloon.

127

I felt as if I was about to slither across the floor and ooze through the gap at the bottom of the window on to the pavement below.

'What have you played there besides – ' she referred to Moray's letter – 'the Earl of Harpenden?'

'Iago,' I said, quickly locating my best voice, 'in *Othello*.'

Mistake!

'Yes,' she smiled forgivingly.

The mohair suit and blue Egyptian cotton also smiled.

'Did – ' she paused, drawing up the guillotine – 'anybody see you in it?'

I hesitated, not for long, but in that split second all the configurations whizzed through my head, like a chess champion on methedrine. Too vain to quit losing, I heard myself say, 'Jimmy Fraser – he came to . . . '

'Did he like you in it?'

'I think so. He said he did – he bought me a drink.' I grinned as if it was a joke, but my timing was definitely off.

She wrote something on her pad. 'Jimmy Fraser, of Fraser and Dunlop?'

'Yes,' I said, 'that's it.' I got up and moved towards the door. It seemed a long way.

'Right, Mr Stamp. Thank you for looking in. Could you leave us a photograph?'

'No.'

As I passed, they both looked sideways at me like tango partners. I hadn't shouted, had I? Maybe 'a little sharp, the delivery, Terence'? I heard Kate Fleming's modulated comment in my head.

' 'Aven't got photos. 'Aven't got around to it yet.' I smiled for my big exit. 'Thank you for your time.'

I took the stairs four at a time, and when I hit the street I stood there for a few moments, breathing heavily. I prayed that she wouldn't check with Jimmy Fraser to see whether I was telling the truth. What would he think? He'd probably drop me like a ton of bricks.

The next day, the very next day, a letter arrived for me at the school from Fraser and Dunlop, 91 Regent Street.

'Dear Mr Stamp, I had a call yesterday from Liz Evette at Associated Rediffusion.'

Shit!

'I didn't realise you intended to look for work so soon. As you obviously are looking, perhaps you could call my office for an appointment so that we can discuss this. Yours faithfully, Jimmy Fraser.'

The signature was confidently scrawled.

God, that morning was long. It simply dragged by. There was no coffee break and it was one o'clock when I finally finished.

Opposite the Gloucester Road window of Dino's was a post office which mirrored the pasta house and occupied a corner. Against its side wall were two pairs of wonderfully designed robust red telephone boxes. God, old red phone boxes were great. There was no pretence of high tech – just the aesthetic of necessity.

When I reached them, they were all in use, but almost immediately one of the twins was vacated. The heavy functional door swung shut behind me on its sturdy leather strap and I was enclosed in my own sound-proofed little world. I put in my four pennies and dialled the Regent exchange, followed by the number I'd already committed to memory.

Brr, brr. Brr, brr.

'Fraser and Dunlop.'

I pressed the silver button A.

'Good morning, Fraser and Dunlop. Can I help you?'

On the other end was the best independent agency in London. I could hear typing in the background. Mum, with her training as a typewriter mechanic, would have known which make it was from the clatter.

'My name is Stamp. I'm calling to make an appointment to see Mr Fraser.'

'Hold on, Sir, I'll put you through to someone.'

There was a click and I was placed on hold. My fellow students exploded past the estate agents on the other side of the road. They looked slightly surreal. Unseen, I watched them. It was like being in my plane tree at home . . . At home; that was a funny slip.

'Hello, I'm Mr Fraser's assistant, Hilda Physick. You are calling for an appointment to see Mr Fraser?'

'Yes, that's it, he wrote me a letter.'

I started to take the letter out of my pocket, then I thought: That's dumb; it's telephone, not television. I knew the letter by heart.

'And your name is?' Hilda Physick asked.

'Stamp, Terence Stamp, like you put on the letter.'

She chuckled. 'Yes, Mr Stamp. Mr Fraser is looking forward to seeing you. When would you like to come in?'

Eleven

An Actor's Life For Me

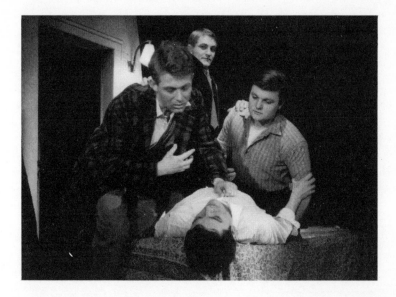

If you enter Regent Street at Oxford Circus and travel south-wards, you save the best until last. To come upon that broad curve, as the steet sweeps majestically into Piccadilly Circus, has always given me a thrill. That's how I saw it the first time I went to the offices of Fraser and Dunlop.

My appointment was for six o'clock on a Friday in July. I arrived early, so I lingered in front of Hamley's windows and made a mental note of a black topcoat with an astrakhan collar in Aquascutum. The sun was dropping that last fast bit. Its rays were reflected in the top-floor windows to my left and, as I turned to cross at the Vigo Street traffic lights, the opposite façade was in shade. The grey stone work looked warm to the touch and one-dimensional, as though an enormous black and white matte photograph had been carefully leant against the building.

I hovered on the island in the middle of the road as the homebound traffic swirled around me. I stood on my toes and flexed my feet, feeling like a matador. Scanning the numerals as I took in the gentle curve of the street, I spotted number 91 a few doors past the arched entrance to Swallow Street.

Fraser and Dunlop's offices were on the fourth floor. Not wanting to pass up a flight of knee-strengthening stairs, I was about to embark on a backwards climb when I heard voices coming down from the mezzanine. Perhaps my knees could wait. I pressed the button for the lift.

The double doors to my right when I stepped out of the lift were solid oak with small panels of bevelled glass halfway up. One panel formed a prism and the sunlight shining into the offices threw a rainbow patch on the wall. Fraser and Dunlop apparently didn't keep traditional office hours (I was unfamiliar then with calls to Hollywood which, because of the time difference, begin at about six o'clock in the evening). Typewriters pounded away thirteen to

133

the dozen. A receptionist took my name and indicated that I should sit down on a narrow seat along the wall opposite the door. On the walls were posters from West End shows. I assumed that some of the featured artists were Mr Fraser's clients.

I heard Mr Fraser's booming voice. His accent sounded more pronounced on home ground.

'He's here? Well, why didn't you tell me?' The familiar figure appeared from a door to my left. He was pulling on a lightweight jacket and his face was a little flushed. He gave me a warm smile.

'Hello, young man, come on in.'

I knew then that everything was going to be all right.

His office was not large and his desk filled the room. He motioned me to sit down. To the right of my chair there was a little table with an assortment of cards and postcards on top. I picked up a card on the front of which was a photograph of a long-haired actor wearing a giant sweater and clutching a poodle. In the background was a front door decorated with a holly wreath. Inside the card read: 'Isn't Christmas a drag.' The face was familiar; I was sure I'd seen him as Pontius Pilate somewhere.

Jimmy laughed when I held the card up. 'That's Frank Thring. He's a great one for cards.'

'He looks funny,' I said.

'Are you leaving the school?'

'Well, I haven't actually thought about it. It's just a bit of a struggle, you know, finding the money to live. I do this backstage job, evenings – '

'But do you think you *need* to finish the course?' he asked in a jocular way.

Thoughts raced through my mind. It was fun being a drama student. It was such great fun. I did love it. I wanted it, but did I need it? I looked at him across the wide desk and said, 'Let's put it this way: if you feel you can get me work, I'll be advised by you.'

He took a filter cigarette from a packet on the desk, then offered the pack to me. I shook my head.

He lit his cigarette and, exhaling, said, 'I can get you work. I'll need you to do some theatre – some rep – in the provinces, as near London as possible. Is that OK with you?'

'Oh yeah – that's OK.'

'You haven't got Equity yet?'

'Nope.'

'Right. I'll look into that.'

'I've got NATKE – the stagehands' union.'

Mr Fraser smiled his cherubic smile. 'You've been a busy young man.'

'You could say that.'

His smile widened. 'I'll need photos,' he said. 'I'll get Max Shaw to take some. He's an actor, one of Joan Littlewood's, but he's a good photographer as well and not expensive.' He must have seen my face fall because he reassured me, 'Fraser and Dunlop will pay for them. We'll deduct it from your salary – salaries.'

It sounded good to me. I nodded.

He said, 'Anything else? Any problems?'

'They've been good to me at Webber Douglas. The scholarship, the bursary.'

'They did a good job, picked the right man. You caught my eye; you're good and you're going to get better. You can repay them best by fulfilling the promise you've shown.'

'I know. It's leaving the nest again, isn't it?'

'Sort of. Look, why don't you finish the third term? Then you will have done eight months. Later you can always study privately. Lots of actors do – big actors.'

'Right. I'll finish the third term – done.'

'I'd like you to meet my partner, Mr Dunlop.' He pressed the intercom. 'Peter, do you have a minute. There's someone I'd like you to say hello to.'

After a few moments Peter Dunlop walked in. He had a military moustache and looked like a huntin', shootin' and fishin' man.

'This is Terence Stamp – Peter Dunlop, my partner. Terence is going to do some rep for us, not too far from town.'

Peter and I shook hands. He nodded his head. 'Right, sounds good, no problem there. Is that your real name?'

'Yeah, anything wrong?' I asked defensively.

'No, no, on the contrary, very distinctive. Just thought I'd ask.' He looked at his watch. 'Good Lord, it's after six. Goodbye, gentlemen.'

135

After he'd left Mr Fraser smiled at me conspiratorially. 'He goes fishing at weekends.'

'I thought he might.'

'How old are you?'

'Twenty. Twenty-one at the end of July.'

'Ah. Leo?'

'Yep. You too?'

'Aye. Is it that obvious?'

'Well, sign of kings. Snobs, aren't we? Only really comfortable with each other.'

'What do you do weekends?'

I shrugged my shoulders.

'You should see some shows.'

'I've seen some – well, from backstage. I've a regular job at Her Majesty's, but I do odd matinées at other theatres during school holidays.'

'Any theatres you haven't worked?'

'Covent Garden – bit of a closed shop there.'

'You have been busy. Now we'll start to make it pay off.' He raised his eyebrows.

It was a deal.

When Jimmy and I shook on it, I didn't quite realise my luck. Jimmy Fraser was a man who had been in the business for over twenty years and nobody had a bad word to say about him. When Jimmy telephoned for a favour no one turned a deaf ear and there ain't much more a young actor who is starting out can ask for. Even in this most fickle of trades, artists had come and gone from Fraser and Dunlop but each and every one of them remained on good terms with Jimmy Fraser. Later I would try to leave the agency myself, but it was like trying to desert your family: easier said than done.

I explained the situation to George Rossiter in his elegant house near the school and left Webber Douglas with his blessing at the end of my third term. By way of celebration I bought a 45 rpm record of Fats Domino's 'Margie', and then made my first visit to Fraser and Dunlop as a full-time actor.

Just as I was about to sit down in Jimmy's office, a telephone call came through from the Theatre on the Green in Richmond. They needed somebody for the role of Private Whittaker in a week-long run of Willis Hall's Army play, *The Long and the Short and the Tall*. Jimmy sold me to them on the phone. The deal would be £12 for the week, plus a week's rehearsal pay. As soon as the arrangements had been made, Jimmy called Equity and fixed a temporary membership subject to my contract at Richmond. Together we flicked through the pictures Max Shaw had taken of me.

'Take these two,' Jimmy said, 'and leave them this one for the programme.'

And so began my first professional acting job. *The Long and the Short and the Tall* had an interesting theatrical history. The Theatre on the Green production was to be directed by Anthony Page, who had been Lindsay Anderson's 'gofer' on the West End production which had made Peter O'Toole an overnight star. Willis Hall had written the lead role of Bamforth with Albert Finney in mind, and O'Toole, unknown at the time, had been offered another lead: Corporal Johnson. According to rumour O'Toole replied: 'I'll play Bamforth, or I'll play nothing.' When Lindsay Anderson later telephoned O'Toole to explain that Albert Finney had been hospitalised with peritonitis, the modest newcomer's response was: 'I'll be there in ten minutes.' As the actor who understudied him for a year remarked, 'Peter was never backward in coming forward.'

So it was that, with O'Toole in the lead, *The Long and the Short* started its West End run at the Royal Court and transferred to the New Theatre. It was a huge success. I could never afford to buy a ticket, and the production carried only a small crew so I couldn't get work backstage, but I used to study the photos outside the theatre, the ones of O'Toole in particular. He was far from having a matinée idol profile and his rugged features and unorthodox looks gave great heart to all of us in a less than classic mode. I saw him once or twice from afar. The first time was at an Old Vic get-together. O'Toole was drunk as a lord, unshaven and wearing baggy, shapeless clothes. None the less, a group of younger actors were quite literally sitting at his feet while he held forth in a clipped Northern accent which sometimes drifted into an Irish slur. Someone told me that he came from Leeds, and resented not having been born in Ireland: if you were Irish and believed that he was too, you were always offered a drink.

The second time I saw him was in the Salisbury pub in St Martin's Lane, which in the Fifties was a watering-hole for all the surrounding theatres. I was in there between shows one Saturday and Peter O'Toole was under full sail, his pale delicate hands at odds with his strong head and wild hair. A frantic assistant stage manager kept rushing in through the side door and pleading, 'Mr O'Toole, please, it's time. We're waiting to start, Sir,' but, unperturbed, Peter just carried on rapping and drinking. After several more increasingly desperate requests, the ASM, who couldn't have been much older than me, grabbed the errant star by the lapels of his Donegal tweed Raglan, stared into the woozy blue eyes and screamed, 'Now, Sir, now.' O'Toole allowed himself to be dragged from the bar, his overcoat flapping open to reveal his Second World War jungle outfit underneath. He managed to drag his free hand along the floor, rubbing the grime into his face as he went: it would have to pass for make-up, presumably. At the same time he did a passable imitation of Olivier's Richard III: screaming for a Fernet Branca all the while and, on entering the stage area, ordering the staff in the flies, 'Take it up, take it up.'

One of the extraordinary qualities of the man was the second set of reflexes which took over as soon as his feet hit the stage. An icy soberness becalmed him until the interval, when he was once again legless and requesting more Fernet Brancas. I thought I could be pretty flash myself until I saw this fella.

Part of the excitement of being in *The Long and the Short and the Tall* so soon after its West End run was due to the play's notoriety. The original cast read like a roll call for the explosion of acting talent of the Sixties. The Samuel French edition of the play includes a list of that remarkable first cast: O'Toole, Robert Shaw, Edward Judd, Alfred Lynch, Brian Pringle, Ronald Fraser and David Andrews. The latter played the part which I was about to tackle: Private Whittaker, the wireless operator.

I needed a Newcastle accent, and Jimmy Fraser introduced me to two Geordies: Delina and her sister Loelia. Delina was the girlfriend of Gary Raymond, whom I remembered catching a glimpse of when I was working backstage on *Expresso Bongo*. Opposite the Savile Theatre, in the last gasp of Shaftesbury Avenue after it crossed Cambridge Circus, were two cafés, both called Velloti's, where I would often take a coffee before the show started. One day I'd been there putting down sand with a girl whom I worked with in the wardrobe department, when I realised that my companion's eyes and ears were no longer with me. An astonishing-looking guy had walked in: he looked like a Romany chieftain, with blue-black hair and riveting, pale blue-green eyes.

'Who is *that*?' she simpered, giving the imposing figure the once-over.

'Somebody,' I said, 'but I haven't a clue who.'

The Romany's eyes cased the room. Then, not seeing who or what he wanted, he turned and left.

Velloti's had been stilled.

'Did you see those minces?' I'd said.

'Touched by a sooty finger,' she'd cooed. *That* had been Gary Raymond.

Loelia graciously agreed to coach me with my Newcastle accent. During the two-week run-up to rehearsals I went to her flat in Westminster every afternoon to work. I found it surprisingly hard-going and George later explained that the Geordie accent was the most difficult to master. Loelia, a working actress, was very strict and took her unpaid task seriously. It was only because of her sheer determination that I turned up for rehearsals with the accent more or less in the bag.

I reported for the first read-through on a Tuesday morning. The Theatre on the Green at Richmond is one of those architectural gems which American tourists imagine to be the epitome of the old English theatre. But, sadly, few tourists ever see the Theatre on the Green as it is situated right at the end of the District Line.

My first impression of the director Anthony Page was that he was a fella who squeezed his toothpaste from the middle of the tube. It couldn't have been easy for him to come straight from a West End hit and have to scale it all down in seven days, but for me it was a baptism of fire. Drama school had been roses compared to this. The actor playing Bamforth was Michael Atkinson and I gathered that he was the resident leading man at Richmond; an extremely competent actor who had opened in a new play on Monday evening and was now starting afresh with us on a new production on Tuesday morning.

The only plus about rehearsing a play in a week is that you don't have time to be nervous. As opening night nears, the working hours become longer and longer, so that when the curtain goes up you are operating on pure adrenalin. I can hardly recall the first performance, except that Bamforth, whose accent in rehearsal I'd thought to be a stage Cockney, took that first-night house by storm.

Although I'd hardly noticed him in rehearsals, the actor who played the brutal Corporal Johnson was quite terrifying on the night. I remember him leaning over the Bamforth character, his face suffocatingly close, and saying, 'I – bloody – do,' with such controlled venom that it made me shiver.

I was too nervous to speak to him, to tell the truth, but one night I came into the dressing-room while he was carefully applying his greasepaint. I opened the cigar box that Moray Watson had given me and took out some sticks of my own, but I couldn't concentrate. I was mesmerised by the Corporal Johnson emerging next to me, and sat transfixed by his reflection in the mirror.

The actor saw my interest and grinned. It broke the ice.

'You're laying the make-up on a bit,' I said.

He rolled his large eyes, and said, 'He's like that.' He could be very chilling.

After that I often saw him walking down the hill from the station. He told me that he'd written a play which had been performed at the Lyric, Hammersmith, although it had only run a few nights. He called himself David Baron, but I later discovered that his real name was Harold Pinter.

When we opened, Jimmy Fraser showed what a good agent he was by filling the theatre with people who might have been instrumental in providing me with more work. I felt guilty about appearing in the play without giving Mum the opportunity to see it, so for her benefit I concocted a story about having joined an amateur group who put plays on in Richmond. Although I didn't really think she'd come, she brought Lynette and Richard one matinée without telling me. Afterwards, they came backstage and I was pleased they'd seen the play but embarrassed that they'd had to sit on wooden trestles in the gods. Later Mum told me how surprised and proud she had been to hear me speak in another accent.

She must have realised at that point that I'd been bitten by the bug, but she didn't raise the subject and neither did I. Seeing me perform in a theatre filled with people who were laughing and enjoying themselves gave my ambition a certain reality for her and, as I hadn't undergone any major personality change, it became less of a vague and threatening idea. Deep down she must have loved seeing all her frustrated theatrical tendencies at last coming to fruition, albeit in her son.

At that time it was a tradition to take a successful show on tour in the provinces after its West End run. No artists in a show ever wanted to go on the road after the main event, so a second company of players was assembled. A touring production of *The Long and the Short*, directed by Anthony Page, had already been on the road. The play was put on in Richmond only when this number one tour ran out of dates and the company disbanded. But, while I was playing at Richmond, Anthony Knowles and Andrew Broughton, the promoters of the tour, hustled up some more dates. Only one role remained unfilled for the tour: Private Whittaker. It was agreed that I should accept the part.

Just prior to my starting rehearsals for this great venture, Baxter and George told me they had decided to go to Jersey to try for the repertory company there. George was obviously getting fed up with the lack of opportunity for him in London and Baxter may have been feeling sick about missing the LAMDA audition which forced him to bide his time for a year. Either way, it left the responsibility of the flat on my shoulders.

I had kept in touch with a layout artist from my advertising agency days. His name was Derek Byard. From time to time, we would meet, see a movie or have a plate of spaghetti in Bianchi's. The thing I liked most about Derek was his humour. He introduced me to the work of S.J. Perelman and I read the great man's books to check whether Derek had committed them to memory.

When I rang Derek to tell him about the flat, he jumped at the chance. But, before I had the chance even to show him the basement, the apartment on the top floor of Number 64 became available without warning. The suite would sleep four, even five, comfortably. The rent was £25 a week. I confided in Derek about my dream of living in the penthouse, and we viewed the place together. He was as impressed by it as me, but we couldn't afford half the rent each. Derek thought a friend of his, a photographer named Ken Wells, might chip in. He rang him. Ken was keen. I went for my first and last meeting with the mysterious Doctor Karp who owned the building. He agreed to us taking the flat.

I moved up on the Thursday. Derek and Ken were to join me at the weekend so I had the place to myself for a couple of days. I purchased a Dundee cake from the pastry shop on Marylebone High Street to celebrate. The move took only two trips up the sedate stairs, cake and all. My belongings looked paltry in the new surroundings. I didn't care. I put on a kettle in the proper kitchen and investigated the layout of the place while it boiled. I wondered which bedroom the leggy Palladium dancer had slept in. We had our own bathroom! It contained a hand-shower attachment, a rare luxury. I thought it was all the polar bear's pyjamas. I made the tea, put it on a tray with the almond-topped cake and carried it into the main room which was a twenty foot by fifteen affair with a wall of windows overlooking Harley Street. I sat on the large sofa contemplating the matching china in front of me, lifting and replacing the quilted tea cosy like A.A. Milne's Eeyore with his burst balloon and empty honey jar. I was sorry that George and Baxter weren't around to share the moment. Baxter especially. With his frail form that as a boy had been schooled to be a jockey, his appearance belied his spirit. There were strong arms beneath those natty Italian jackets. While he'd been hauling himself up by his bootlaces, he'd had the energy to drag me along with him. I would have made it eventually, but without him it might have taken me years.

I thought about the previous tenants, and how Gilly had prevented our meeting them. She'd succeeded in confining us belowground, possessively flaunting her acquaintance with the famous upstairs dwellers and their starry visitors. Petula Clark, Judy Carne, Roger Moore and Dorothy Squires all trod the stairs up to the penthouse suite. What did they do up there? How did people behave in the rarefied penthouse atmosphere of fame?

A key turned in the Banham lock. Derek had come to visit on his way home from work. He took in my solitary feast and gave me a wink. 'Man lives as sparks fly upwards,' he quipped.

My brother Chris had by now left school. He hadn't taken a regular job, preferring temporary work. He and his mates had purchased an old Daimler hearse in which they cruised around visiting the local dance halls. His mates had the makings of an extremely tough lot (the 'strongman' of the group was later to serve time for robbery and GBH) and Ethel was so worried that she asked me to have a word with my brother.

I invited Chris to see my new drum. I had been letting go a bit with money, adding the odd luxury to my diet, and on the morning that Chris visited, I prepared Cornflakes with fresh strawberries. He was impressed.

We talked about my forthcoming tour. I let him in on my secret: I aimed to make my mark in showbiz before telling Mum and Dad. He promised not to mention any of this at home. I then asked him what he was going to do with his life.

'I don't know,' he said.

'Well, what sort of things interest you?'

'Nuffink.'

'Come on, Chris, there must be something.'

'There ain't.'

'I'm sure you'd like a load of bread,' I suggested.

'Not much – I got enough. It ain't everyfink, you know.' He sort of wrinkled his forehead, inviting philosophical dialogue.

'OK. Putting work and stuff aside, where are you? What do you do with yourself?'

'Go out with the lads.'

'To do what?'

'Cruise around, lig about – dances and stuff.'

'So your only real interest is . . . '

'Girls – that's . . . Yeah, girls.'

'What sort of girls?'

We'd finished the Cornflakes and had wandered into the passage. Now we were squatting on the carpet in the hall.

'Just girls. You know – any. They don't have to be beautiful. I mean there's more of the others.'

I stood up and walked down a few steps of the inner staircase, speaking to him through the banisters. 'But, if you could have your pick, what type are you into?'

Chris bit the nail of his index finger with the tooth he'd loosened one night at Fairbairn Boys' Club when, hanging on to a gym rope, he'd launched himself from the inner balcony. His contact with the wall opposite had been the talk of Fairbairn for weeks. 'Dancers,' he said, after some time. 'Yeah, that's it, ballet dancers. They 'ave them 'ard muscular legs.' He looked exhausted at the prospect.

'Sadler's Wells.'

'Wot?'

'That's where you should be – on the stage staff.'

'Why?'

'It's a ballet company. You could do what I've been doing: working backstage.'

'What for?'

He was normally extremely quick on the uptake but I spelled it out for him.

'In a ballet company there are one or two star dancers. The *corps de ballet*, however, is made up of about thirty dancers, some boys, mostly girls, all about sixteen to twenty-five years old. They work so hard and so long that they don't meet guys outside the ballet. Most of the ballet boys like each other. Most of the girls like boys, but don't meet any. You can't get hold of boys you don't meet. A lean and horny tearaway like you could do well in such company. All you need is a union ticket. You could use mine for the moment; pass yourself off as me. Call in backstage today, number 19 bus.'

Chris was hired immediately. I received only one phone call to say that I had screwed up on the timing: he'd joined Sadler's Wells during the opera season.

'I'm holding my own, though,' he told me. 'Some of them souperanos have great lungs.'

A few weeks later, as stage manager OP side, he left with the ballet touring company. The Grey Wolf had started his run.

Twelve

Caine Cometh

The Duke of Argyll is one of the four pillars of Soho. It stands on the corner of Great Windmill and Brewer Streets, and, like the great pillars of Islam, it embraces all faiths. At the end of the Fifties, the few hundred square yards which constituted Soho accommodated every conceivable nationality huddled under the one eiderdown: trade. A brisk stroll along a few streets could fill a basket to satisfy the most travelled palate. In those days there were no strip clubs in this little inland island. The Windmill – 'we never close' – was known to me only for being opposite the best salt-beef sandwich bar in town. Jack Spot – rumoured to be a gangland boss – amicable offered me his place in the queue when I tried to bunk in once. Fortunately for my digestive system, I didn't know who he was until the owner told me on my following visit.

The first floor of the Duke had an all-purpose room available for hire and it was here that the cast of *The Long and the Short and the Tall*, the second touring version, gathered to knock the production into shape for its final stretch.

Our director, Jerry, was Irish. He introduced himself but, never having directed anything before, he didn't bother to introduce us to one another. We plunged straight into a read-through, and as soon as we started I could tell that we had some heavy-duty guys on board. I kept my head buried in the text and made little attempt to distinguish between my fellow actors. At the end of the read-through, an assistant named Howard fetched some tea and the tension eased somewhat. I've noticed since that whenever a group of performers come together for the first time their energy switches to 'on': the result for me is usually a kind of haze. I often can't distinguish one from another.

It wasn't until after the tea break that I heard a deep voice with an unmistakable South London accent annotating our director's verbose explanations. Jerry read the stage instruction: 'There are several loud bird calls and on the third one the door bursts open and in comes Corporal Johnson followed by . . . ' and the resonant voice drawled, 'The door bursts open and in the shape of a big bird on comes Corporal Johnson.'

This improvisation was followed by a high raucous laugh which was so infectious that the rest of the cast laughed as well. Everyone, that is, except Jerry.

I turned to identify the owner of the voice. He was a strapping young man with a head of unruly blond curls. His nose was sharp, and the set of his jaw gave him an air of insolence. But the most arresting feature was his eyes: they were large, hooded and blue. Those minces, combined with pink-rimmed eyelids, white-blond lashes and a kind of glaze that myopic people get when they're not wearing specs, gave the impression that he was about to sneeze.

Michael Caine. He was playing Bamforth. The part had been conceived with Finney in mind, and had catapulted O'Toole to stardom, but for me the definitive Private Bamforth was Michael Caine. For a year he had understudied O'Toole, literally waiting in the wings while the star was being hauled, legless and roaring, out of the Salisbury and on to the stage. I never heard Michael Caine say a word against O'Toole but in private he could do a wicked imitation of Peter's nasal Leeds-Irish-Cockney rendition of Bamforth.

When I met Caine he was twenty-six, and already a veteran of the Korean War. Accredited as one of the best marksmen in the British Army of the Rhine, he had returned to Civvy Street unscathed. He'd had a hard time in showbiz, playing extras and walk-ons. His biggest film was *A Hill in Korea* in which he doubled as a technical adviser, but if you study the film and blink more than once you may not catch him at all. When he'd come out of the Army, Mike had found a job as an oily rag in an obscure provincial repertory company and married the leading lady. It didn't last long.

(When he later moved into the flat in Harley Street, the police often came to pick him up for failing to pay his alimony, although the poor guy didn't even have the price of a pair of specs most of the time. None the less, this didn't stop him mopping up the magistrate.

'Harley Street! Rather a swish address for someone with no money, isn't it, Mr Caine?'

'Look at it this way, Guv. Think of all the money I save on fares coming to court.')

Like me, Caine loved the idea of making movies, but had fallen foul of the English system which does not consider actors worthy of film until they have proved themselves in the theatre. Taking the job of an understudy in *The Long and the Short* had been a gamble for Mike; a gamble which, true to his run of luck, he'd lost as he hadn't made it onstage. He knew as much about the play as anybody and could have directed it in his sleep better than dear old Jerry, although none of this was apparent in his modest attitude.

Mike was cool towards me during rehearsals but, since all the actors were somewhat older than me, that did not strike me as odd. I comforted myself with the fact that I'd already successfully played the role in Richmond, and I figured that the less they knew about me, and my lack of experience, the better.

Rehearsals finished on a Friday, and the Saturday night before we were due to travel to Nottingham, our first port of call, Willis Hall invited the entire cast for a drink at his house in Ebury Street, girlfriends welcome. I took along a dancer-model I'd met while doing a commercial for Knight's Castile soap during my week at Richmond. She had that alluring combo of paper-white skin and black hair. I was having a thing about bow ties at the time, and proudly sported a floppy purple velvet number which my Aunt Julie had made to my specification.

When Michael Caine arrived he was accompanied by the most gorgeous girl I had ever set eyes on. He introduced the ravishing creature as Marie Devereux. I thought I might pass out on the spot and, judging by the stunned silence that greeted her entrance, most of the other guys were having the vapours as well.

When the cast assembled at King's Cross Station next day, Caine marshalled us into two adjoining carriages with an air of 'I've done all this before, lads'. I stayed close to him, figuring that he would always be at the centre of the action.

It turned out that Mike was the sole survivor from the initial tour; the rest of the pioneer cast were working elsewhere when the recall came. Sitting opposite Mike was Tim Pearce, an actor of about my age, maybe a little older, who doubled as an ASM. He had the head of a Paul Newman and the physique of a Burt Lancaster; I assumed he had only just come into the business. Together with a tall and rangy Don Quixote-type called Howard Daley, he was understudying the entire cast.

Tim and I were sitting with our backs to the engine, and Mike held the floor from his centre seat facing us. He rarely glanced my way and I felt left out but not uncomfortable. Inevitably, the chat got around to girls. Mike talked about places without bothering to identify or explain them; I assumed they were pubs. He described a chain of events which occurred in 'the Buxton' involving an American girl, whom he referred to as a 'bird', a term now commonplace, but rare at the time. This bird was in the habit of frequenting the Buxton at lunch-times wearing sheer black silk stockings. On this particular occasion she had stretched her legs out, resting her high heels on the seat of a stool in front of her. Caine, sitting near by, had a view which, he said, had him 'biting the knobs off a chest of drawers'. He concluded, 'She was with a geezer called Brook Williams, Emlyn's son, otherwise I would definitely have given her a john bull – definitely!'

There was a pause.

As the floor seemed open for comment, I said, 'Roberta – was that her name?'

Caine's heavy-lidded beadies swivelled in my direction.

'In *West Side*, was she?' I added.

Mike's mouth opened slightly, his tongue pressed against his top lip. 'Yeah, that's it. D'ya know her, then?'

There was something challenging in his tone. He paused, energy coiled.

I backed off a bit. 'Yes, I do, as a matter of fact.'

'Well, like, do you know her well?'

A toothy grin flashed at the others. Ah! I got it. OK. I waited. Mike sucked in his nostrils, making his nose narrow, hawk-like.

I said, 'Well, I don't like to boast about these things, but yes, well, very well, as it happens.'

Caine's face split with pleasure. 'You're pulling my leg,' he said.

'Nope, but as you're obviously keen to pull hers, she's called Roberta Keith, just moved to Cornwall Mansions, side of Madame Tussaud's. I'll give you her number. The first time I met her she was complaining that English guys were so groovy-looking, but they just didn't screw.'

The thicker I laid it on, the more Mike was enjoying it.

Finally, amidst laughter, he said, 'I bet you changed her mind?'

'I did my best.'

'So! You're one of the lads, then?' With a king-sized grin, he continued, 'Blimey, I thought you were a poof.'

He leaned forward and extended a meaty hand, as though apologising for his having jumped to the wrong conclusion.

I was now included. We became a band; a troupe of stroller-players. All my life, without knowing it, I had wanted this. I felt like Pinocchio striding out with strains of 'hey-diddle-de-dee – an actor's life for me' sounding in my ears.

Things went from good to better as soon as Mike discovered I was a real East Ender. When, after several weeks on the road, I accidentally let slip that this was my first professional part, I gained immense stature in his eyes. He was more impressed by my chutzpah than anything else. He glowed with enthusiasm and told me: 'You've got more front than bloody Woolworth's,' as though he was relieved to find a fellow Londoner, a lad after his own heart, standing up to the invasion of actors from the North.

Once again I had landed on my feet.

On this tour we were booked into those theatres with the greatest capacity, usually in the middle of provincial towns. I had always wanted to visit Nottingham, our first venue. It was where Errol Flynn had vanquished the Sheriff and won the hand of Olivia de Havilland, and it was my old friend Lee's dream of nirvana: a place where the streets flowed with girls from the tobacco factories at a ratio of five to one – or so we imagined.

On our arrival on the Sunday evening, the first thing we did was to make our way to the stage door for a first sighting of the digs list. Caine explained to me: 'It's essential to be quick off the mark before the good digs get snapped up.' He had change at the ready for the stage-door pay-phone and was armed with a few loaded questions for prospective landladies. How big were the rooms? What were the other boarders like? Was the grub any cop? Last, but certainly not least, was the house averse to outside talent – female company? From town to town, the digs situation varied enormously, ranging from great to duff; a common factor being landladies who generally liked 'theatricals' and had a field knowledge of their needs. My first set of digs in Nottingham spoiled me. I think I may have been my landlady's first lodger. I was given a full English breakfast, sometimes with field mushrooms the size of saucers. If I'd been out carousing and slept late, she brought me breakfast on a tray, a fact which didn't crop up in conversation with Tim and Mike until after we'd left town.

Mike said, 'In bed? Breakfast in bed?'

Tim said, 'You jammy bugger.'

'I think she might have been after a bit on the side, my old son,' Mike added.

'Oh, I don't think so; she was happily married,' I explained.

'You never know until you've tried, son.'

Mike ran amok with sexual theory even when sitting down.

'What would you have done, then, Mike?' asked Tim.

'Well, I definitely think it was worth letting the eiderdown slip. I mean eggs, bacon, and mushrooms specially; all good popcorn gear.' He turned to Tim and, pointing a thumb at me, said, 'I see we're goin' to have to take this lad in hand.'

Jack Smethurst (Taffy), who'd joined our little group, and was in the habit of practising his Welsh accent at odd times, said, 'Doesn't look like he's doing too bad on his own, look you.'

'Yeah, but it's that Orphan Annie bit. I've met blokes like that before. It takes so long, that little-boy-lost caper. It's no good on the road.'

Mike could go on like this for hours. I was lapping it up.

Jack was a terrific performer and a really up guy. He liked a drink, to say the least, but we'd hardly begun to appreciate his talents when he had to leave. I never learned whether it was the offer of a better job or some family crisis that whisked him away. Two nights before he left, we all wound up in the Peach Tree, the pub opposite the stage door, to wish Jack well and to welcome his replacement, a real Welshman called Johnny Rees.

1 David Baxter in Hyde Park

2 Gloria with her Jack Russell

3 Fairies in the stalls at Webber Douglas.
Penelope Keith is wearing the hat.

4 Kathy Breck as 'the Wall' in *A Midsummer Night's Dream*

5 Kim Carlton as Titania

6   Gloria as Hermia and me as Lysander

7 My first professional
photographic session

8 Brother Chris, who
became the Grey Wolf

9   Derek Byard, David
Baxter, me and Ken Wells
(*clockwise*)

10   Marie Devereux

11 Mike Caine and Robert Shaw in rep together

12 Mike Caine in *Danger Within*, one of his early films

13   Doug Sheldon

14   Me and Doug

Halfway through the evening, I said to Mike, 'There seems an awful lot of pretty birds in here tonight.'

Mike slipped out his National Health specs which had only one lens, held them up to his eye, had a quick look around, and stuck them away again. 'I think you're right, old son.' He leaned over to Jack and mumbled, 'Lot of crumpet tonight, don't ya think?'

Without a pause, Jack spoke to the nearest couple of girls. 'Want to go to a party?'

The nearer of the two girls smiled and beckoned to some friends who came over. 'Where?' one of the girls wanted to know.

'I haven't decided yet,' said Jack. 'Who's got a nice house we can use?'

A blonde, a strawberry blonde, answered, 'We could use mine. My parents are away this weekend.'

'Right,' said Jack, 'that's settled, then. Where do you live, love? Mike, take care of this little darling; she comes with the drum. Got lots of friendies, have you, love?' Jack leaned over the bar to the barmaid. 'Listen, Peachy, bottle of gin, bottle of vodka, bottle of Scotch and brandy to go.'

Most of the cast in the pub were suddenly leaving like rats from a ship that's not sinking. Before I knew it, and hardly believing our luck, we all found ourselves in a smart detached house on the outskirts of Nottingham. Bobby Darin's 'Dream Lover' was on the polished wood radiogram, Mike was riffling through the LPs for long-term material and Jack was setting up a bar in the adjoining dining-room. It was a bare fifteen minutes since I had called Mike's attention to the superior quality of the female company in the pub.

It was the best party I had ever been to. It had everything. Walking into a room to find girls trying to peel Tim's shirt off happened so many times that I thought I'd developed double vision in both eyes. At one point I bumped into Mike in the main dancing area and remarked on this phenomenon.

'You noticed that as well, did ya? I'm glad you told me; I thought somebody had spiked my drink.'

I was busy pursuing a gossamer sylph called Tessa, when the hostess, who was draped all over Mike like a tent (I don't know how she got him to smooch; he was a notorious non-dancer), whispered to me as I passed, 'She's an iron butterfly – dance with that one over there,' and pointed me in another direction.

I was on my way when Jack zoomed across my path.

'We're out of booze, darlin', I'll organise a whipround and you get along to an off-licence and stack up.'

I said, 'You must be joking; it's gone one o'clock.'

'You're right,' he said. 'Pity to spoil the fun, though; I'll think of something.'

About an hour later Sinatra was singing 'Only for the Lonely' when Jack sashayed alongside me dancing 'Only for the Grotesque'. He offered me a refill.

'Not bad,' I said, taking a sample. 'I thought we were out of hooch?'

'Necessity, Mother of Invention, old chap,' he managed to drawl.

He appeared smaller than usual. I looked down and saw that he was sagging at the knees. His hand was flexed, as though expecting contact with the floor at any second. I tried to steer him to a chair but he wouldn't move.

'Jack, come on. Own up; what is it?'

I figured by the state of him that he'd located the family's supply of methylated spirits.

'Oh, nothing to worry about; all kosher stuff.'

'I thought the house didn't run to a cellar?'

'Better,' said Jack, sliding nearer to the carpet. 'Come wiv me – show you, s'great.'

I put a steadying arm around his shoulders and he took off like a chimp. In the spacious dining-room he pointed out a neatly arranged collection of miniature liqueurs, now seriously depleted in number.

'The one I think is doing it,' he rasped, 'is Parfait d'amour. It's mauve. There was rather a lot of them.'

'Oh, Jack, you haven't whipped all the guy's collection?'

'I'm not *that* stupid. Every *other* one.' He rolled off back to his punch-bowl.

I took the lissom Tessa a glass but my amour was far from parfait that night.

We travelled north on Sunday, leaving a forlorn Jack behind at the station. He was a bit tearful.

'Still pissed, I suppose,' said Mike later.

Hugging me, Jack said, 'I'll see you about.'

'I don't even know where you live,' I said.

'Weybridge, but don't worry, darlin'. If we stay in the business we'll bump into each other.'

Thirteen

Timing? I Nicked It
From Bob Hope

E n route to Edinburgh, at about four o'clock, Mike said, 'This feels like a tea train. Let's cut along to the buffet car before all those toffee-nosed gits in first class grab the seats.'

It was indeed a train which served tea; another luxury of the road. Mike and I sat at a table for two next to the window. We were travelling through Border country and the views were epic. Again I experienced the stimulating 'actor's life for me' feeling.

Mike bunged the waiter half a crown straight away and said with a wink, 'Extra tea cakes, John, and don't go easy on the butter.'

'Well done for me,' I added.

As the train slowed to take the bridge over the Tweed, we munched on our high tea. I tried heather honey on my toast and Mike gave me some tips on comedy timing in general and on playing the role of Whittaker in particular.

'Timing? I nicked it from Bob Hope. I reckoned he was the guvnor. His material's not always up to much, specially them road movies, but he always pulls the laughs. It's the timing does it. The line, the pause, the laugh. It looks easy – but it ain't. There's a lot of laughs you're missing. It's mainly the accent.'

'It's no good?'

'It's too good.'

A beefy finger reached across and pressed my hand to the table. The sun was just going down, catching low clouds on the way. Rays spilled through the carriage windows, highlighting the hairs on his wrist which were almost white.

'It's too good. It's Geordie, you see.'

'But in the script – '

The finger tapped my hand. I shut up.

'It's just a script. Actually, it's a good script. But *we* make it real. On paper it's linear. Our bit is to give it dimension. We are

159

up there; our sphericals on the line. David Andrews cracked Whittaker so that, when they didn't have tears in their eyes from crying, they had 'em from laughing. He's gormless, see; a gormless northerner. You're making it harder on yourself by not letting the audience in on it straight away.'

He lifted his hand, picked up the silver-plated pot, and raised it a few inches in front of him. Seconds later, 'John' arrived with more hot water.

'Nothing wrong with your gormless Geordie, but if you make 'im just northern you've plugged straight into a tradition going all the way back to George Formby. You only have to open your mouth and they know instantly. You've got 'em. Gormless northerner – you wouldn't actually have to change anything. I threw out things Peter O'Toole changed because I'm doing it real Cockney, and kept stuff that was genius, of course. I'm not trying to prove anything, outside of being a terrific Private Bamforth. O'Toole used to say, "And in the blue corner weighing in at seven stone ten, the Wakefield weakling." Wakefield, see. He and David Andrews worked that out. Laugh for Bamforth; sympathy for Whittaker. We both win.'

'When do you think I should start?'

'Straight away – Scotland, see. Tomorrow.'

'It's a difficult – '

'It's not – it's nothing. You tell the boys, specially Lenny [my big scene was with Leonard Fenton who played Smith], what you're doing, and then do it. They won't care. Up here they relate to Corporal MacLeish. By the time we get to Bradford, you'll be perfect.'

I felt flattered by his interest. I would have tried anything he advised. His experience of the business was vast: six whole years.

In Edinburgh Johnny Rees, the actor who'd replaced Jack Smethurst and a fellow tea addict, helped me explore the finer tea houses of the city. He was nursing an ulcer and took his tea weak with plenty of milk.

Princes Street was elegant compared with Oxford Street. It was obvious why the Scots were so proud of it, although many of the old shops have been ruined since. A hamburger chain has now been granted a prime site but in September 1959 Princes Street was resplendent in its Highland glory. One shop, William Jamieson & Son, had one entire window display devoted to honey. I had never seen honey in a comb before. Johnny bought us each a slice of honeycomb and we munched on it as if it were ambrosia. That was how honey seemed to me then. I'd changed my performance, as Caine had advised. I had anticipated real problems, but it wasn't at all difficult. Laughs followed, as Mike had predicted, and my confidence grew with each performance. On the Tuesday after our opening night, the *Scotsman* published a big picture of the entire cast above a favourable review in which I had my first mention. I wrote to Mum telling her about Scotland and despatched a copy of the review to Jimmy Fraser. The next time I spoke to him on the phone I could hear him purring with pride, not about my mention but because I loved his capital city.

I was staying in digs near the King's Theatre and my landlady, recognising the signs of a visitor falling under Edinburgh's spell, started to give me haggis for breakfast. To my astonishment I found it delicious, which was just as well because if I didn't eat it all in one sitting the leftovers were sliced and fried with bacon the following morning.

Jimmy had negotiated a fee of £16 a week for this tour. All train tickets were paid for by the company, so I could live well on my salary. Mike, who commanded higher fees and, as he confessed when I discovered him checking the attendance at the box office, a percentage, always picked up the tab in cafés, or sometimes treated me to a packet of cigarettes, usually Gauloises which were his favourites at the time.

'They put stuff in the others to keep 'em alight. It's no good for yer; stops you getting a hard-on.'

I was soon hooked, but whenever I tried to return the compliment he declined, saying, 'There'll be time enough for that.'

After Edinburgh we travelled to Hanley, the pottery town. The train sped into cloud and we didn't emerge for a week, but the theatre was the most modern we'd played, and had lifts up to the dressing-rooms. However, the auditorium was too big for us to fill and, worse, the Hanley streets were bereft of girls. It was only on the Friday, the day before we left, when the cast were invited to the Wedgwood factory outside town, that we realised where they all were. I bought Mum a Wedgwood blue teapot but, in true working-class tradition, she thought it was so beautiful that she never used it.

By now I was receiving regular mentions in the provincial dailies and I could feel the character of Private Whittaker beginning to flesh out. I recalled what Kate Fleming had told me on my last Sunday visit before leaving London.

'The voice is something unique. It is like a fingerprint. Everyone's is different. But it is more than a fingerprint, because it's dynamic, more subject to change. You can tell more from someone's tone of voice than from the expression on their face. When you start to develop your voice, it's like putting money in the bank: even when you're not adding to your balance, what's there is growing, gaining interest. The voice never slips back; you never lose the work you've put into it. Every time you breathe fully and speak from the diaphragm, it invigorates the voice. I don't just mean more breadth, more depth. You bring a radiance to it the way a violinist brings vibrance to his or her fingers. It is the magnetism of the voice that holds people, gives them the confidence to listen, to leave themselves open to you. Every time you help your voice, it helps you. And it gets easier. Don't worry; it does get easier.'

On the sleeper back to London, Mike and I took a bunk each. John Trenaman, who played Corporal Johnson, jibbed in and roughed it on the floor. We spent the day in London and caught the boat train to Dublin in the afternoon. Any excitement I might have felt about leaving the British mainland for the first time was quelled by the choppy crossing from Holyhead to Dun Laoghaire. Although I came from a long line of sailors, I was as sick as a dog from the moment the boat set sail across the Irish Sea. Next morning I tumbled off at the other end, the colour of a shamrock, and vowed never to travel by boat again.

Mike hailed a cab and told the driver: 'Take us to the Gaiety Theatre, and go steady: me mate's a bit fragile.'

'Rough crossing, was it?' The driver turned round to have a look at me. 'I'm not surprised,' he said. 'It's like that most of the time. I know somewhere that'll fix youse up in no time at all.' He slammed the car into gear and shot off as though I was in need of a blood transfusion, ignoring traffic lights altogether.

After we'd sped across several that were blatantly against us, I asked, 'Wasn't that light red?'

It was then that I heard that memorable line.

'Sure it was. You see one, you've seen them all.'

At the theatre he jumped out of the cab. Instead of opening the trunk to help us with the luggage, he scuttled into an alley at the side of the theatre and beckoned us to follow. Tim gave us a look – in for a penny, in for a pound – and we followed the leprechaun. He stopped outside the stage door, but, turning his back to it, knocked on a much smaller door opposite. After a second or two the door was opened a crack. The driver mumbled something in a thick brogue and we all trooped into a big shiny pub: Neary's. There were only a couple of customers but it was business as usual.

Our guide was already at the bar.

'Yer man's a bit queezy here from ter ship. Have you got anything for that?'

The barman screwed up his red face and looked at the clock on the wall.

'I can't serve you now, it's Holy Hour,' he said with a wink, 'but if you sit yourself down I'll give yer a drop of porter while you wait.'

He turned to fill up a thin pint glass with pale brown foam, slicing the head off from time to time with a piece of wood tailor-made for the job. The big clock behind the bar read ten to eight.

I said to the barman, 'Couldn't we get into trouble? I mean, it's before opening hours.'

'I shouldn't give the po-leece any mind, lad.'

'Why not?'

'Well, it's like this, yer see. That's the chief of po-leece over there.'

He pointed down the bar to a man who raised his glass to me.

'Welcome to Dublin,' said the cop.

We didn't get first crack at the digs list that day.

Frank O'Keefe, a fellow student at Webber D whom I had admired from afar, came to see the show at the Gaiety. Afterwards he presented himself backstage and proceeded to introduce us to his world. What a world it was, and what conversation! I often become exhausted in the company of people who don't draw breath, but in Dublin I found I could listen for hours and feel exhilarated. During one of these conversations I asked about the habit Dublin drivers had of ignoring red lights, and discovered that on the whole driving wasn't taken too seriously in Ireland, a country which did not even insist on a driving test before issuing a driver's licence. I thought they were pulling my leg when they told me that a licence could simply be purchased at the post office, but I was intrigued enough to try for myself. The next day I filled in an application form, giving my Dublin landlady's address, and handed ten shillings over the counter. The driving licence was issued on the spot. I was thrilled. I used it for a year, which meant that by the time I needed a valid British licence to insure my own car I could handle a motor well, albeit in a rather getaway style.

I felt at home in Dublin, and I often passed for a local. If I was on the street with Mike or Tim and we gave any girls more than a casual glance, they would lower their eyes and cross themselves. We laughed about it but it did make me feel dangerous to be on the loose.

When it was time to return to the mainland, Jerry gave me special dispensation to travel to Manchester by air. Before I left the rest of the cast, I arranged to meet up with them at the train station before journeying on to Bradford for our next date. That plane trip was my first flight, and it gave me a God-like feeling.

I arrived in Manchester on a Sunday morning with six hours to kill. The city centre was like a morgue. I was suddenly over-whelmed with a longing to be back in Chadwin Road for lunch. I kept telling myself that it would only be a few hours before the others arrived, bringing with them all the warmth and zest of a company on the road, but waves of loneliness kept swamping me. I felt as though I was the only person left on earth. Not finding an open tea shop or café anywhere, I made my way to the Library Theatre in the hope of finding a weekend 'get in' in progress. But the circular building and the surrounding neighbourhood were bare and deserted. In my desperation for human contact, I had a wild notion of calling my boyhood chum Bernie Wilson's sister Shelagh. She was a fashion model with her own agency in Manchester. Bernie had talked about her so often that I felt I knew her well and, in any case, I'd worn her husband's cast-off monogrammed shirt until it disintegrated. I scanned the local telephone directory and rang the promisingly titled Shelagh Wilson Model Agency. There was no answer. I gave up and sat on the stone steps of the library.

A great silence enveloped the streets. It wasn't like the quiet between two sentences or that moment before the telephone rings: it was just unqualified stillness. I could move my head and alter my view, or shift my bones on the chilly, spotless steps and hear the rasp of my flannel trousers as I moved; the sound didn't break the stillness.

I have no idea how long I sat there – I had lost all sense of time – when suddenly I felt someone near me. I turned, vaguely aware of a stiffness in my body, and saw a youth standing a few paces behind me. My first impression was that he wasn't too tightly wrapped. He was neatly turned out, after a fashion, in a heavy broken-diagonal suit which was well cut but tight and shiny like his shoes. His teeth were irregular. His five o'clock shadow would have been the envy of spaghetti western make-up artists the world over. Single hairs of differing lengths had escaped his razor, giving his top lip a unique look.

He grinned lop-sidedly and said in a Mancunian accent, 'You sitting there.'

It was a statement of fact, not a question. Not wanting to seem rude, I swivelled towards him and stood up.

Although he was a step above me, his face was lower than mine. 'What yer doing?'

'Killing time.'

He nodded. His instant acknowledgement showed that he was no stranger to the condition. We stood a few paces apart: two extraterrestrials from different planets.

'Do you know anywhere I can get a cup of tea?' I asked.

'Aye.'

'Is it near here?'

'Aye,' he said again. 'Shall I show you, then?'

'Sure,' I said.

We started to walk through empty streets, chalked pavement squares of old hopscotch games passing beneath us. Where did everybody in Manchester go on a Sunday? After a while we reached a row of terraced brick houses, blackened by years of soot from coal fires. There was no sign of a tea shop. It wasn't until we came to a halt in front of a house no different from the rest that I realised he'd brought me to his home. He put a pasty hand through the letter-box and retrieved a piece of string at the end of which was tied an iron key. I remembered a similar device I'd used in my childhood when visiting Granny Stamp in Poplar. The hallway was dim and its walls were papered with lincrust which looked as though it had been varnished. He led me to the kitchen at the back of the house, where he put a kettle on the stove.

The kitchen had that warm homely atmosphere shared by all well-used kitchens. I would have been happy to stay there, but a battered tin tray was produced and we went upstairs to his room, which was small and cluttered. I kept expecting something untoward to happen. As I watched the lean, white hands fixing the tea, I understood that I was being exposed to an intimate ritual, a glimpse into a private world I sensed was important, but I knew not how. I had the impression of an intelligence that was at odds with the person in front of me. I'd had similar feelings when looking into the steady eyes of a newborn child.

It appeared that my young host was a tailor. From his cupboard he brought forth things he'd made, lengths of material and odd-ments that had caught his eye. He asked me whether there was anything I had ever wanted and hadn't been able to afford.

'Lots,' I said.

'Something special?' he wanted to know.

I remembered a story about the young Cary Grant which Baxter had heard when he'd worked backstage at the Victoria Palace during the last season of the Crazy Gang. Some of the Gang had known Cary since the days when he'd been the 'top boy' of a circus tumbling act. Often his dressing-room was so small that Cary Grant, or Archie Leach as he was known then, received guests and potential employers in the passage outside, somehow contriving to give the impression that his dressing-room was a place at once private and splendid. On such occasions the future film star always wore a well-cut dressing-gown, the ultimate in chic. Since hearing this story, I'd had a dressing-gown fixation, and regularly combed Jermyn Street seeking a garment which would have won the approval of the great Archie Leach. When I told my host about my preoccupation he was delighted and said that he would make one for me. After taking my measurements, he insisted on escorting me to the station, all the way to the platform. When we were within twenty or thirty yards of the other members of the cast, who by now had arrived, he just vanished into the crowd of passengers milling about the station. It was a memorable experience, but I couldn't figure out why.

Several months later a sealing-waxed parcel arrived in the post at Number 64. The dressing-gown inside was a perfect fit. It was black with red shawl lapels, expertly finished with twisted red and black silk cord. I was so proud of it that I wore it to my dental appointment with Mr Heiderman, who rented a floor of our building. The poor man was so offended that he banished me from his surgery and refused ever to treat me again.

On the train to Bradford we passed the signposts to Wakefield: the town of which my Private Whittaker was now a famous son. I was extremely nervous by the time the train pulled in at our destination a few minutes later. Mike assured me that I needn't worry; before I'd joined the company he'd played nearby Leeds and everything had been hunky-dory – not, he added, that the audiences compared. Leeds was known to have one of the best audiences in Britain, whereas W.C. Fields was reputed to have said of the Bradford audience, 'When the curtain went up I thought they'd left the iron down.' (The iron was a fire prevention barrier that was lowered during the interval.) Later the same evening he allegedly said, 'For my next trick I'll make the whole fucking lot of you disappear.'

But events boded well on our arrival in Bradford. Mike and I settled ourselves in a spotlessly clean house near the theatre where Mike caught me washing my feet in the bidet. It was the first bidet I'd ever seen and I quickly deduced from its shape and size that it was some kind of foot bath – a story which Mike Caine dined out on more than once after I got my break. Only breakfast was provided at our digs, but over the road from the Alhambra stage door was a fish and chip shop where you could buy a piece of fish and a generous helping of chips in a greaseproof bag for a shilling. That solved the problem of our evening meal.

As Mike had predicted, as soon as Private Whittaker was identified as being local, a ripple of pleasure and sympathy went through the house, and during my big scene in Act Two I could feel the audience solidly on my side. Such is the power of local patriotism.

Mike and Tim were on the look-out for Bradford talent but, although the streets were filled with northern beauties, neither of them was having much success. Tim reckoned that they needed to adopt a system, and Mike agreed. 'A system. You're right, me old son. We've got to get organised.'

He looked at me sideways. I could see the cogs turning. He was unusually quiet as we made our way to an underground coffee bar we'd heard about. It was five-fifteen when we arrived. The place was empty.

'Right,' said Mike, 'we've got time to sus it out before the after-work deluge.' He pointed a large thumb at me. 'Laughing boy 'ere's got that *Woman's Own* appeal, so he's the bait. We'll put him – ' he looked around the room, taking in the lighting – 'here, by the juke-box.' He turned and gave me his cobra look, a technique which caused temporary paralysis in women. 'Now, you're not to talk, get it? Whatever happens you're to stay stumm. You just do that little-boy-lost thing but no dialogue. Got it? Tim and me will put the sand down. You're in a silent movie – drop that left eyelid like Valentino, but no chat.'

Tim laughed.

Mike pursed his lips and drew himself up to his full six foot two. 'Now, Tim, you're over by the door, and I'm here.' He went over to a shadowed alcove and pulled out his specs which still sported only one lens. A strip of Elastoplast held one of the arms together. 'I can clock what's going on with the bins on, and as soon as anything dishy takes the bait – ' He whipped off his National Healths and nipped back to the juke-box, as though blocking a stage move. 'Now, Tim, the minute you see any possibles give him a wink and you,' he pointed at me, 'put some soft record on, so as to give the old profile some back-up.'

I'd been studying the selection on the juke-box. 'What about "Sing Little Birdie"?' I asked.

'Yeah, that's 'orrible, that'll do, but don't put it on till Tim gives you the nod. Right, cappuccinos all round – got enough tanners?'

Obediently I checked the few sixpenny pieces in my pocket.

At five forty-five people started drifting in. Mike sat in the alcove wearing his accident-prone specs, giggling at my efforts to droop an eyelid. Suddenly Tim stiffened by the door and I dropped a tanner into the Wurlitzer. As 'Little Birdie' hit the turntable a group of three – two brunettes and a blonde – came down the stairs into the room. One of the brunettes curled a lip at the music and came straight at me, with the other two in tow.

'Did you put that on?' she demanded. The eyes, nearly as dark as her black woollen stockings, flashed aggressively.

I was about to say, 'It's a free country,' or something equally suave when Mike and Tim moved in on either side of the trio.

Mike silenced me, saying, 'I told you to push the buttons carefully, Tel. They don't work like they do in London, these old machines. – Sorry about that, darling. Now, what's your pleasure?'

The saucy one turned her head and gave Mike the once-over. Specless, and lighting a filter Disque Bleu, he slid his eyelids halfway up and matched her look over the flame of his lighter. The cobra was about to strike.

' "Great Balls of Fire" all right?' he said, reaching for Jerry Lee Lewis on the selector.

The blonde was eyeing Tim's shoulders. He was wearing an oatmeal slipover with a cut-away boat neck which exposed the full glory of his trapezius and gave the pitch of his head an ancient Greek look. Tim's only problem was that when a girl fancied him he didn't have any choice in the matter. I could see that neckline being clawed down at any second.

'You want to feel my traps, baby?' I heard Tim say.

Mike tilted his head like Cary, the voice hit its low register. 'So you're Tina, Tina.'

Me? I looked into the green eyes of Chloe – and was in love.

Fourteen
Clark's and Cornflakes

Getting a crush on the road can be hard on the system. The Sixties hadn't officially arrived and the Beatles were yet to show how little separated North and South. Chloe, or Claudette as she'd been christened, was torn between continuing our friendship, thereby risking the perils and glamour of London, or restricting it to a brief interlude, thereby retaining all the cosy assurances of family and old friends. I understood her feelings only too well, and we reached a compromise. We exchanged photos; we promised to write. She came to see me off; we held hands on the platform. She'd bought a new lipstick, bright and light. I wished she hadn't. Our farewell kiss took place to the accompaniment of jeers of envy from the cast who were already on the train.

As the train pulled out, I watched the slim figure turn and walk away and I remembered the long rides on our way to the Brontë territory and the strolls across the moors where Heathcliff had roamed. I hadn't used the wiles of a travelling player although I had ached to investigate her fineness. I had been half-conscious of the fact that any pressure on my part could so easily push things out of shape. I'd hesitated, waiting for a guiding nudge. None came.

On the train, Mike had saved me a window-seat facing the engine. He beamed at our travelling companions and said affectionately, 'What about our boy, then?' He was like a proud elder brother.

Later, on the way to grab a high tea, he said softly into my ear, 'Can't win them all, son. It's the trying that's the lark.'

We hit Bournemouth next. Mike, whom I always suspected had a kind of Semitic know-how, quipped after looking round, 'If there are only four million Jews in the world, why are they all in Bournemouth?'

'Lot of bread here,' I informed him.

'You can say that again.'

It was an extraordinary squeaky-clean resort unlike any seaside I'd seen before. It was more how I imagined Switzerland to be.

My Uncle Harry, the dancing-champion wood-machinist, regularly took his holidays in Bournemouth, staying in sea-front hotels and going to dances twice a day. Even so, I was intimidated by the place. So was Mike.

'They're not going to take too kindly to some of the dialogue in the show,' he warned me.

'What are you going to do, then? Water it down a bit?'

'No, I'm going to really stick it on 'em.'

He spoke with such relish that it stuck in my mind. Although I didn't follow the reasoning at the time, it stood me in good stead years later.

During our week at the Bournemouth Pavilion, Errol Flynn died. Mike and I drank a toast to him when we heard the news.

'Safe voyage, Errol, old son,' Mike said.

'Yeah, first class all the way,' I added.

It was a great moment of loss. Flynn had been a part of my life. He had always been there. All his expressions, especially the famous grin, were etched into my memory. I had seen *Captain Blood* and *Robin Hood* so many times during my boyhood that I'd thought of Flynn as forever young. It took a while to face the fact that he was no longer alive.

Unexpectedly, a midweek matinée was scheduled. We hadn't given one before, but presumably the many retired residents of Bournemouth made afternoon performances profitable. Curtain-up was at two-thirty. Everything was going along normally when Tim appeared at Mike's door to say that it was already two-thirty and Harry, who played Corporal MacLeish, wasn't yet in his room! The rest of us hurriedly assembled in Mike's dressing-room. We carried only two understudies. Tim Pearce covered Mike Caine and one half of the cast; Howard Daley covered John Colin and the other half. In an emergency the role of MacLeish was Howard's responsibility. However, we didn't carry any spare costumes and since we had been on the road Jerry had called only a couple of understudy rehearsals. As these were conducted with the two actors playing eight parts between them, it is hard to imagine the format, let alone what use they were for the would-be players.

Howard was duly summoned from the wings. He entered the room meekly and Jerry explained his fate. If only it could have been Tojo, the Japanese prisoner, who didn't have a line. I've never forgotten the look on Howard's face; in fact, it has been the trigger for a recurring nightmare I've had over the years. In my dream I've been contracted to revive the role of Alfie. I have convinced myself that the marathon role is embedded in my memory, unshakeable and irremovable. I haven't bothered to relearn it. The tension of the first night will force the lines to re-surface. I'm on stage waiting for the curtain to rise . . . but my mind is blank . . .

As if poor Howard didn't have enough on his plate, we couldn't find any boots large enough for him. There he was on the side of the stage, arms and legs protruding awkwardly from the uniform, trying to force his feet into a pair of tiny boots.

Mike was standing behind me and whispering, 'I *will* marry the prince, I will, I will.'

The curtain whisked up, the jungle birds on the tape recorder began squawking away and we all tumbled onstage. To be fair, the new Corporal MacLeish didn't do at all badly in the first act, although he was uncertain about the moves. The rest of us desperately sought to steer him but could do no more than give the barest of body signals. Howard's traumatised feet would move only once the rest of his body was in motion which made him resemble a lanky Max Wall doing an eccentric dance. Mike, who knew the piece inside out, threw in ad-libs like, 'You're not going to tell me it's my turn to guard the Nip, are you, Corporal?' and, 'Look at me when you speak, will you?' He would then mouth Howard's next line out of the upstage side of his mouth.

Eventually the curtain came down on the first half, and during the interval our absentee actor bowled up. Harry Caddow had been sunbathing on Bournemouth beach when suddenly he had a funny feeling that he should be somewhere else. Harry was a little older than the rest of us. All his experience had been in the provinces, but he knew the business and took great pride in his craft. He'd never missed a performance before and the shame was written all over his creased face. Although he tried to make light of it, he was desperate to go on for the second act during which Corporal MacLeish carried the long opening

175

exchange with the Sergeant, while the rest of us supposedly snoozed.

'What are you talking about, you Scots git?' demanded Mike, lapsing into Bamforth. 'Go on for the second act! What'll they think? You're the incredible shrinking corporal?'

Harry exploded more easily than he might have done had he not felt so guilty. 'What is the lad going to do with all the dialogue?' he screamed.

'He's learning it now,' I chipped in.

'He canna learn it in fifteen minutes.' The role had taken Harry weeks to learn.

Mike said, 'Well, he can bloody try. Any rate, it's better than Mutt and Jeff in two acts.'

John Colin, with statesman-like calm befitting his stage rank of sergeant, sized up the situation and sought to diffuse it. 'Harry, Howard's *got* to go on. You get behind the flat and give him the lines as best you can if he gets stuck.'

There is a phenomenon known in the business as 'corpsing'; that is, succumbing to an irresistible urge to laugh or giggle during a performance. Some players can exercise a degree of control over it; others have no control whatsoever. Some performers, usually male and of an inebriated disposition, go out with the intention of setting others 'off'. (I once heard of a notorious Irish joker who went to the trouble of fixing a sausage to his underpants. During the play he turned upstage, unzipped his fly, whipped the banger out in front of the unsuspecting leading lady, and cut half of it off with a pair of prop scissors. She apparently passed out.) No formal rules apply to these japes, but it's considered bad form for the instigator to be facing upstage (with his back to the audience) if his victim is looking downstage in full view of the audience.

Everyone positioned themselves onstage and the curtain went up. I was upstage for the second act, as a look-out at one of the windows. Offstage, Harry began scampering about on his knees behind the flats, stage-whispering the dialogue to Howard who delivered the lines in a faltering, out-of-sync and decidedly Scottish accent. Then I got the giggles. I felt the laughter welling up in me like bubbles in shaken cream soda. I started to shake. Lenny Fenton, at the other window, caught it from me, and it spread like a contagion. As soon as the other slumbering soldiers 'woke up', it infected them, too. Trying to conceal my face, I pushed my head out of the window to compose myself and take some deep breaths, only to catch sight of Harry's red features shining up at me like a new penny. I quickly withdrew my head, praying for sobriety, but almost the whole cast seemed to be in various stages of hysteria. Mike was astride a bench next to the Japanese prisoner. He looked pretty straight-faced but his bayonet, shaking like a leaf, was a dead giveaway. Taff was downstage on his hands and knees. It looked as though he had been trying to get up, but as I watched him he just collapsed and rolled over like a ladybird on its back. Corporal Johnson tiptoed upstage in slow motion, clutching himself as though in the final throes of diarrhoea. Fenton and I stood by the windows, panting like two dogs. We were all ludicrously trying to face away from the Sergeant and Howard who were sitting downstage. Howard had taken his boots off and the stalwart John Colin was reciting MacLeish's lines as well as his own in some inspired schizophrenic monologue.

The play was meant to end with the dud radio suddenly sputtering into life and a Japanese voice starting to taunt us, at which point we would all turn to face the radio and freeze into a tableau before the curtain was lowered very fast. But, at the end of this memorable midweek matinée, Howard, being onstage instead of at his usual post in the prompt corner, wasn't able to give a precisely timed curtain cue. The entire cast stood frozen onstage, with open mouths. We looked like a collection of Edvard Munch paintings. Suddenly realising that the curtain wasn't coming down, Jerry, who had been in the wings, came to life and hit the light switches. We were plunged into darkness. Caine, assuming that the curtain had already come down, hurled his bayonet on to the floor in a fury and bellowed, 'Fuck me!' We reeled offstage and then tumbled on again for our bow. I don't know who was more stunned: the Bournemouth audience or us.

Our next venue was Sheffield, followed by a week's break in London. Mike had an infection in one of his eyes and spent much of his time at Moorfields Eye Hospital. I dropped in to see Jimmy Fraser, who said that he was trying to get me seen by Jack Cardiff who was about to direct a film of *Sons and Lovers*. He was looking for a newcomer to play the part of Paul. I knew the book and I got it into my head that this part was for me. I was so green that I told Jerry I would be quitting the play in Cambridge, even though we had a few more bookings lined up after that. The realities of surviving as an actor hadn't yet hit me, and I'd never considered the possibility of being out of work for a long stretch.

Mike arrived in Cambridge with a black patch over one eye. The hospital had told him that the eye had probably become infected from the stage make-up and Mike therefore announced that he planned to go on wearing the patch.

Jerry objected, and a heated discussion followed, with Mike holding his ground.

Finally, Jerry said, 'Well, wear your usual make-up, but don't put anything near the bad eye.'

Mike couldn't believe it. 'Wot, and come on looking like a bloody Bonzo?'

He wore the black patch.

(That was my first inkling of Mike's phobia about his lashes. He would take great care to mascara them whenever he performed but it would never have crossed his mind to wear make-up in the street. Later, when Mike and I were living in Ebury Street in Belgravia, he came bounding up the stairs one day, holding two small glass bottles and announcing triumphantly, 'This is it! Someone's finally cracked it.'

'Cracked what, Mike?'

'The eyelashes. Look, a dye! You put it on yourself.'

'Does it work?'

'I dunno. I thought it'd be worth a try.'

He rushed up to his bathroom on the top floor. Ten minutes later he came downstairs. The stuff had worked all right, but in his haste to transform his long lashes Mike had omitted to protect his eyelids. He really did look like a Bonzo for a couple of days.)

When I told him of my decision to quit the play because I felt certain I would get the film role, Caine gave me his famous old-fashioned look, but said only, 'Hope you get it, then.'

The tour ended for me on a Saturday night. My brother Chris drove down to Cambridge on his motorbike to catch my last performance. On his way from London he fell from the saddle in a rainstorm and tore the whole of one trouser leg. He knocked at the door of a nearby house and borrowed a dozen safety pins, so that when he arrived backstage he looked like the first punk, about twenty years too early.

Mike didn't offer to exchange phone numbers after the show. He just told me he'd see me about. It was a bit of a let-down being back in London without his wisecracks.

I went to see Jack Cardiff at a flat in Green Street. He was courteous but didn't snap me up instantly. I was sure that he was seeing other actors and at some point I would get recalled. But that didn't happen.

Some days after my interview, I was wandering down Curzon Street. It was a street I had been attracted to ever since I'd read the Edgar Wallace 'Just Men' books. I often bowled about the neighbourhood. On this particular day I was walking east from the Park Lane end when I saw walking towards me a familiar couple: the girl dark-haired and beautiful on the arm of an imposing blond guy, the triangular black patch still over one eye. With his uneven gait, his pea-jacket and bleached desert boots, he cut an outlandish figure. He would have been more at home at the helm of a tall-masted schooner than on a London street.

However, they both seemed pleased to see me.

'Hello, sunshine, we were just talking about you,' Mike told me.

Marie said, 'We've been to see a film at the Curzon – *Hiroshima Mon Amour*. Mike was saying he'd meant to tell you about the cinema; it's his favourite.'

Mike had taken over my education, loaning me Ian Fleming paperbacks, and giving advice on what perfume to buy for the ladies. Now he said, 'You should give it the once-over, the film and the cinema. Film's got an original love scene, rare, and they might be knocking down the Curzon soon to put up an office block.'

I was pleased. It sounded like he might have been missing his willing novice. 'Hey,' I said, 'I didn't get that Lawrence film. Can you believe that?'

Mike shook his head and clicked his tongue.

Marie said, 'For someone so smart, you can be such a berk!'

'Give us yer number; I'll give you a buzz,' said Caine.

I've often wondered how things turned out for Marie Devereux. We were about the same age and became good friends while she and Mike were together. Later she went off to Rome as Elizabeth Taylor's acting double in *Cleopatra*. I saw Marie once in Hollywood, but we lost touch with each other after that.

The first time Mike came up to the flat and I showed him around, he remarked that there was plenty of room.

I said, 'It sleeps four, easy. If you want to crash here, you can.'

A few days later Caine moved in. He travelled light. A typical stroller-player, he appeared to have little concern for possessions – or, if he did, at this point in his life it hadn't surfaced. He had few clothes: in fact, he wore what little gear he owned. When he arrived with his belongings, he took off a shirt and several sweaters before unpacking a suitcase which contained mainly books and long-playing records. A small record player and portable typewriter completed his luggage.

Whatever I had felt about Mike's guided tour of the provinces, seeing London through his eyes was even better. He hadn't acquired rich habits. He'd been exposed to them but not long enough for treats to become necessities and he was able to get by on very little. His chief motivation was to stay in the business, so as to be ready for his break when it came, and he'd acquired no small degree of mastery in the field. His attitude allowed him to live like a lord and he set out to teach me to do the same. When we earned wages, we invested them.

Mike rarely used money on transport, preferring to walk. As it was the only kind of exercise he indulged in, a good pair of shoes was essential. They had to be hard-wearing as well as good-looking enough for auditions or interviews. After spending long years trying to solve the footwear problem, he finally discovered the Clark's desert boot.

In the Fifties, the desert boot was manufactured solely for export and was only occasionally made available in reject form from the factory outside Glasgow. Canny Scottish actors had discovered the Clark's boot and invested their 12/6d to excellent purpose. The boot, because of its cheapness, comfort and apparent indestructability, had acquired a certain chic. It was considered acceptable in almost any social situation.

The Clark's boot had only two flaws: first, the crêpe sole slid on wet fallen leaves; second, and more serious, was the in-built obsolescence of the inner sole, on which the foot actually rested. This part of the shoe was constructed out of a material which, when the boots were most loved and looking their broken-in best, cracked completely across the widest part of the foot.

In later years, when Clark's became available to the local populace at full price, the in-built weakness was still present. Many people wrote to the manufacturers to draw their attention to this single flaw which stood between them and the perfect footwear, but the flaw persisted. In the days of the great walkabouts – Aldermaston, and other memorable rallies – people coped with this problem by cutting out their foot shape from breakfast cereal packets and inserting the cardboard into the boot. Cornflake Clark's, we called them.

Neither Michael Caine nor I worked for some time after the tour of *The Long and the Short and the Tall*, and Mike's rationing techniques started coming into their own. The penthouse soon became a financial burden. When it was obvious that Derek and Ken were only too willing to take on the whole kit and caboodle, Caine and I found a furnished house at 12 Ennismore Gardens Mews. As it was too expensive for just the two of us, Mike contacted an old chum, a part-time actor named Tony Calvin. Together we made the move to Knightsbridge.

Fifteen

Not Wanted on Location

Number 12 was above two garages. The property was of doll's-house proportions, but we were so keen to live in a mews house which both Mike and I thought was the epitome of chic th it we didn't consider how restricting a lack of space might be. In any case, Tony had a regular job with a script-printing company and was out most of the time. He took the single bedroom and Mike and I shared the double with twin beds. The rent was £12 a week.

Partly to celebrate our move to SW7 and partly to give ourselves something productive to do until the big acting breaks came our way, Mike and I decided to collaborate on writing a film script. Our first effort was entitled *You Must Be Joking*.

One aspect of Mike's master-plan was to take over the British film industry, so that he would be able to make the kind of films he admired. As I was now included in this ambitious manoeuvre, Mike raised my sights a bit by introducing me to the National Film Theatre. I don't think he was ever a member but there were other ways of getting in, and, once inside, the seats weren't expensive. Our excursions into the world of Fellini, Truffaut or Fritz Lang usually included an excellent crusty cheese roll and cup of tea which passed for lunch and supper.

One of the great charms of flat-sharing with Mike Caine was that he seemed naturally able to make the best of every moment. When he woke up he would look out of the window, assess the day's character and make a plan.

'Right, it's a shiny, upper-middle-class day. You have first bath; I'll make some breakfast. Then we'll stroll to Harrods and mingle with the other idle classes. You can cruise the pet shop and I'll see what new books they've got. Then we'll cut through the parks to Leicester Square and read all the papers in the library. How much money we got?'

We would pool our resources.

'It'll be nearly lunch-time by then. We'll nip into that gaff in Whitcomb Street before the luncheon-voucher lot get loose.'

He knew an assortment of cheap and amazing cafés. My favourite was the one in Whitcomb Street. It housed a dashing Victorian steamer which produced the best puddings I have ever tasted. They were made with the most delicious gelatinous pastry and cooked individually. We would have steak and kidney, or sometimes rhubarb or apple with custard. If we were flush, we'd have everything.

Mike also introduced me to the wonders of Indian cuisine. One of his favourite haunts was the Curry Centre in Soho, where he instructed me in the correct way of eating beef vindaloo. 'Don't drink any water until you've eaten it all, no matter how much it burns. If you drink halfway through, it's worse. You can't finish.' Needless to say, we never started anything we couldn't finish.

After lunch we would listen to the latest sounds in the booths at HMV, browse for hours in Foyle's or visit new building sites which Mike had got wind of. He held the theory that contemporary architecture reflected the state of the nation and was intensely interested in what was being done to South London. We sometimes strolled to the Elephant to keep an eye on promising developments there.

Our plan for the day always incorporated several showbiz haunts where Mike could pick up information about possible productions currently in the pipeline. Mid-afternoon we would hit the best tea room in London. Housed in Gerrard Buildings, it was called Le Grain; everybody knew it as 'not wanted on location' because it was always full of out-of-work 'crowd' (film extras). If our finances hadn't stretched to a proper lunch, we'd have a lamb sandwich, then linger over milky tea in a glass, changing tables until we wound up at Mike's favourite. Being at the back of the room, against the wood-panelled wall, it gave the best view of the action.

We'd be home around six, by which time the heater would have heated the water for the second bath.

'And then we'll make some phone calls and set up things for tonight.'

Caine didn't have any representation and relied heavily on the personal network he'd built up. I often asked him why he didn't get himself an agent. He never gave a straight answer until I offered to introduce him to Jimmy Fraser, whereupon Mike confessed that he had once written to all the established agents. Nobody had been interested except Jimmy, but during the first few weeks of being on Jimmy's books Mike had taken a job looking after a rifle range at the Festival Gardens funfair in Battersea Park. Jimmy had seen Mike working this side-show and thereafter stopped calling him. Later, when I took the matter up with Jimmy, he didn't remember the incident, but Mike had a phobia about approaching any agent and it was some time before he let Marie introduce him to hers: Bill Watts. Mike liked Bill and his wife, but was self-conscious about being represented by an agency mostly known for its glamorous girls and starlets. Mind you, when Mike and Marie separated, Mike brought home some corkers he'd met in Bill's front office.

I loved living in Knightsbridge. Our mews was the most pictur-esque in London, overlooking the grounds of Holy Trinity Church, immediately behind Brompton Oratory. This splendid little row of seven or eight cottages was approached through a Roman arch and the street was cobbled. In summer, residents festooned their house fronts with trees in tubs, and gardeners in vans came to refurbish the window-boxes. This Tom Thumb stretch was always quiet and peaceful. I had a lingering fantasy about purchasing one of these mews cottages when I made my fortune. When I confided in Mike, he said we'd have a house each, side by side, when we were running the British film industry. A few months later, one of the cottages was purchased by Alec Guinness. Well, at least that showed there was no real prejudice against actors.

After being out of work for six months, I followed up a call from Jimmy Fraser and found myself at the Arts Theatre Club in Great Newport Street. The evening before my audition Mike gave me his system for an on-the-spot reading.

'A basic mistake all young actors make is to overlook the fact that you get the job in the office. We're so busy worrying how we'll play the part if we get it that we screw up that first reading and don't get the job. I have therefore worked out a thesis from the ceiling of my vast experience of not getting jobs which I will treat you to if you're interested.'

'Fire away.'

'If you get a butcher's at the script before you go in, just familiarise yourself with the dialogue while you're waiting. Because showbiz is so disorganised, and the actor is generally a last-minute consideration, you only get a look at the script the second before you're expected to read aloud. This is where my system scores.'

'I'm still all ears.'

'I can see that. Now, the minute you get your mits on that script, you memorise the first line or couple of lines your character has to say. Most directors read the other part – most of 'em fancy themselves as performers. Now, while they're reading their dialogue, don't look at them, 'cos that's when you're learning your next line, so that *you* can look *them* in the eye when you're delivering. What could be easier than that?' He spread his hands out like an Italian waiter presenting the house speciality.

'It's all split-second timing, though, ain't it?'

'It always is, but I've taken the bother to analyse it, which gives me an edge.'

'What if it's a long speech?'

'Works the same: remember the first sentence; say it, looking him in the eye; look away so he knows it's a deliberate pause; then look down, grab the next line, and same again. Like falling off a log. Always resist the impulse to rush. It's never bad to pause at a reading; in fact, it gives you class. Makes you seem confident.'

'I'll try it tomorrow.'

'Do that.'

Mike's scenario unfolded as he'd said it would. I was shown into a little room just off the theatre foyer. Two men were seated and there were a couple of scripts on the table.

The older man said, 'I'm Robert Cartland, this is Jonathan and you're – ' he consulted a list – 'you're Terence.'

'I'm Terence.'

I sat in a chair facing them. Jonathan offered me a script. The director picked up the other one.

'We'd like you to read Ben,' he said.

The title peeped through a little cut-out rectangle on the cover: *A Trip to the Castle*.

The part was that of a Teddy boy who tries to rape the unconventional daughter of shabby nobility during a paid excursion through their stately home. I can't say I appreciated the text, which, as one critic put it, 'seemed to be in praise of the idiosyncratic life of the unique individual', but I figured that the only 'juve' worth playing was Ben Irwin, the rapist. When I was recalled and offered the role of one of Ben's stalwarts, I took a tip from Peter O'Toole and told Mr Cartland that I would play the gangleader or nothing. The gamble worked and I was given the part. A hoodlum in a velvet collar. I was to be paid £10 a week. There was live incidental music by Johnny Dankworth, and lots of mumblings about Shavian fantasy and shades of Christopher Fry. Most of it was over my head.

I didn't feel as buoyed up as I had thought I would be, considering this was my first West End production. My spirits were particularly dampened when, on the Saturday evening before we opened, I went to see the last performance of the play we were to follow into the Arts. It was called *The Caretaker*, and was written by my acting chum David Baron, now Harold Pinter.

My main intention had been to reconnoitre the auditorium for sound during a show, but I was instantly engrossed by the play and performances by Peter Woodthorpe, Donald Pleasence and Alan Bates, the latter of whom was all bruised insolence. As I walked home after the play, I was assailed by a kind of envy. It was the feeling of being left behind. Something new was happening and I was missing the bus.

A Trip to the Castle opened on Wednesday 1 June 1960, and the only solid audiences we had were for that night and the public dress rehearsal the day before. (After that business was so poor that most nights you could have fired a shotgun through the house without hitting anyone.) When the curtain went up for the dress rehearsal, I was so nervous that the inside of my mouth dried up completely and for the first scene I felt as though my throat was stuffed with sandpaper. After the show, I tried to unwind in the bar upstairs. Susan Franklyn, who had been in the same year as Samantha at Webber D, came in. Susan was as striking as Samantha; with the sort of figure that Vargas liked to draw, she was not difficult to look at. She had been in the audience. Although at school she hadn't paid much attention to me, she seemed set on making up for that now. The evening with Susan hadn't been anticipated in my master-plan. My mind chose to be on other things for a change.

On opening night I recalled George Chakiris's trick and inserted a partly sucked sweet into the side of my mouth a minute before curtain-up. Writing in the *Financial Times*, the critic, T.C. Worsley, said, 'I must single out Mr Terence Stamp for special mention, since he has the relaxed contemporary manner to very life.' (By permission of Spangles.)

In the cast was an actor named Douglas Sheldon. His parents were carnival people, and although Doug didn't have a private income I'm sure they helped finance his foray into showbiz. He was generous to a fault, and often chauffeured Mike and me to appointments, more often than not with us wearing Doug's natty reversible cord driving coats. He had the rugged good looks of a young Hardy Kruger and owned a white Austin Healey Sprite which he drove as though he were a Formula One ace. We often went buzzing about the West End with the top off, sleeves rolled up and driving gloves turned down, imitating Jimmy Dean, and listening to Duane Eddy.

Doug Sheldon's arrival in our circle brought a definite improvement to our wardrobe. Mike and I had put together an outfit which we called our audition piece; it was a selection of clothes which would pass muster at interviews and auditions. Because of the difference between our builds, we had a problem getting clothes to fit both of us. Garments had to be a little large for me to allow Mike to squeeze into them.

We heard that Albert Finney had been cast in *Lily White Boys*, to be directed by Lindsay Anderson at the Royal Court. Mike had auditioned unsuccessfully and when I found out that they were looking for an understudy for Finney, the Cockney lead, I thought I should test Lindsay's knowledge of Cockney realism a second time. In his audition Mike had donned our outfit and sung 'How You Gonna Keep 'Em Down on the Farm?' I followed in the same gear, giving a rendition of 'I've Got a Lovely Bunch of Coconuts'.

The keeper of the flame leaned forward in the stalls, resting his chin in his hands. I felt sure he was the sort who wore the shoes that reminded me of Cornish pasties. After a long pause, he said, 'Ye – e – s.' There was another pause. 'Thank you. We'll let you know.'

'I don't think his idea of Cockneys is the same as ours,' I reported to Mike.

'Well, we'll be able to check out his realis-mo when it opens, won't we?' said Mike.

We'd recently moved our operation from Le Grain in Gerrard Street to the Kenya Coffee Bar in the King's Road. Now that Mike had an agent doing the legwork for him, it wasn't necessary to be continually scouring the West End, and SW3 was definitely becoming the place to be.

'I've only been sitting here for twenty minutes and I've seen half a dozen real crackers,' he said, his eyes on semi-permanent 'cobra'.

'Watch it, you're becoming a right voyeur,' I warned.

'*Voyant*, you mean.' Mike spoke passable French which he'd taught himself, loping off to Paris on the boat-train when things got on top of him. 'Voyeur has sexual connotations,' he explained. 'I'm just a witness.' He grinned and waved a long arm at the waitress. 'She ain't bad either, speaking as an impartial observer, you understand.'

Lindsay Anderson did not 'let me know'. Months went by with both Mike and me out of work – 'resting', as we called it. Before I started acting, I used to think that 'resting' was just a camp term dreamed up by some indolent thespian. Now that I wasn't working I understood what a major part confidence played in one's ability to perform. It made sense to employ a term that at once disguised and dignified an unpleasant fact. I have always experienced a kind of emotional exhaustion after I have been doing a play, even for a short run of a week. I have never appeared in a successful long run, with a run-of-the-play contract, and I don't know how other actors cope. Sir John Gielgud once told me that he only feels 'settled' when doing a lengthy stint, but he was unable to explain to me how he kept himself emotionally 'topped up'. Whenever I've found myself in a run of any duration, the problem of making the play and performance real night after night becomes a nightmare for me.

After 'resting' unwearily for a while, I secured a job in Canterbury with the rep at the Marlowe Theatre. The first part I played was Ralph in Robert Anderson's *Tea and Sympathy* – a role which required me to strum guitar and speak with an American accent. I had done neither before and set to work on both. At the first read-through, the lady who was playing the lead role of Laura said to me in the tea break, 'Have you played this part before, son?' It took the wind out of my sails. I suppose it was a back-handed compliment.

It wasn't until the Tuesday morning after *Tea and Sympathy* opened, when we started rehearsing the following production at the crack of dawn, that I realised what a luxury it had been to have an entire fortnight to come to grips with a dialect. Jean Holness, my leading lady, was the resident actress at the Marlowe and had probably been on this treadmill for months. Our next play was (again!) *The Long and the Short and the Tall*. This time I played Bamforth. If I hadn't known the play backwards I could never have learnt the words in a week, let alone taken the stage and acted the part.

Many people outside the business wonder how actors manage to learn all those words. I don't understand, and cannot explain, this mysterious process, although the facility can be developed and exercised, like a muscle, and you do get better at it with practice.

The critics in Canterbury were kind to me during my season there. I received terrific notices for my Bamforth, but provincial rep is a lot different from a number one tour and deep down I knew that I had brought to the part nowhere near as much weight as had Mike Caine. He and Marie actually came to Canterbury to see the show. I was so nervous about their being in the house that the guts dropped right out of my performance that night. The other actors walked all over me, especially an assistant stage manager who'd done his idea of an oriental make-up for the non-speaking role of the Japanese prisoner and kept directing knowing smiles out to the audience, as though he was playing Yum Yum in *The Mikado*.

Caine was furious and gave me a dressing-down about it afterwards. 'That guy is just a wanker; he'd never get on under normal circs, only in a small company with not enough bread for a full cast. You're the lead and you've got to have enough clout to pull guys like that into line. Don't have any scruples about doing it, either. Just knock 'em flat on their arse. You should have grabbed that little squirt's face when he was playing out and held on to it until he stopped. Good actors don't do it; it's only arseholes with no confidence who need to upstage and tread on laughs. Any prick can do it.' His face was pale with anger; it was easy to see he'd had to cope with more than his share of arseholes. He finally smiled, put one arm around Marie and with the other tugged the front of the jungle shirt I was still wearing. 'And, remember, young Terence,' he advised, 'if you're going to go for it, you've got to make it stick.'

Not long afterwards Mike got a part in Pinter's new one-acter, *The Room*, at the Royal Court. He was beginning to make it stick all right. I continued trudging around the reps: back to Richmond to do an undistinguished thriller, the name of which I've consciously blocked from my brain, and out to Windsor for a couple of months. It seemed an age before Jimmy Fraser told me that Wolf Mankowitz, the writer, was trying his hand at production and was about to launch a new play entitled *This Year, Next Year*.

I'd first met Wolf Mankowitz when I worked backstage at the Savile Theatre on his musical *Expresso Bongo*. He'd grown up in East Ham and had a soft spot for fellow East Enders, so he agreed to let me read for the male juvenile. When I landed the part, I thought: This is more like it; perhaps it's even the break I've been waiting for. The three leads were to be played by Pamela Brown, Brenda Bruce and Michael Gough; John Dexter was to direct. We rehearsed in London before starting a short tour prior to the West End opening.

Before I left town Mike took me to meet David Andrews and his wife who had a flat in Earls Court. I was glad to meet the actor who had played Private Whittaker in the original West End production of *The Long and the Short*. Mike spent most of the evening reminiscing with David while I chatted with another guest, a playwright named John McGrath, who was even leaner than I was. This casual meeting was another example of my being in the right place at the right time and not knowing it. Only when I glanced back did I become aware of the fine links that drew me to my real big break.

Sixteen

A Window Opens on Golden Square

*T*his Year, Next Year was set in Edinburgh, home town of the playwright, Jack Ronder. The play told the tale of two sisters who shared a flat, and their eccentric neighbour, a violinist, who lived upstairs. I was the musician's beatnik son, a would-be poet. John Dexter, the director, had been amicable in rehearsal and had me playing the role with a Scots accent which I based on the comedian, Chick Murray.

When we opened at the Lyceum in Edinburgh we had good press and full houses. Everybody in the cast was buoyant except Pamela Brown, who was far from confident about the play or its title. She suggested that if *This Year, Next Year* went to London the critics might retitle it *Sometime Never*. She was particularly kind to me, however, even saying that I reminded her of the young Richard Burton who had appeared with her in his first West End role in *The Lady's Not for Burning*.

'You should be in movies like him,' said Pamela. 'Burton knows which side his bread is buttered. He was already making weekly deposits in his post-office book when I knew him. If I were your age that's what I'd be doing, dear. Movies! There's no future in theatre, no proper audience. It's all coach trade nowadays.'

Our next venue was at the Opera House in Manchester. I bumped into Brenda Bruce at the station and we shared a carriage. I remembered how Mum and I had listened to her in Terence Rattigan's *While the Sun Shines* on the wireless. Now I got a kick listening to Brenda talking about the part of Mabel Crumb, the role she'd played in the original production with Michael Wilding.

Brenda is a Londoner. She told me her folks were publicans but she'd always been hooked on the theatre and had persuaded them to allow her to join the Birmingham Rep when she was fifteen. On the first day she had arrived at the theatre wearing a

197

very tight skirt, platform shoes and thick pancake make-up which failed to disguise her teenage acne. Stewart Granger, then leading man at the Birmingham Rep, had taken one astounded look at her and said: 'Hell's bells, whatever have we got here?' Brenda had broken down in tears. Homesick and uncertain, she had written to her parents every night. After a few days Mr Granger had taken the hapless girl under his wing and even offered a remedy guaranteed, he'd said, to cure her spots. She'd documented this change of heart in her daily missives home, innocently explaining to her mother that the awful actor had turned out to be quite nice after all. 'He's even going to give me something for my pimples,' she wrote. 'It's called a good fuck.' Two days later Brenda's folks had arrived to take her back to London.

When I reported at the Opera House on the Monday after our arrival, John Dexter invited me to take a stroll with him. As soon as we were clear of the building he started to explain that the West End theatre owners who had travelled to Scotland to see the play had one major reservation, and that reservation was me. They thought I was miscast; I was eye-catching in the wrong way. They wanted him to find a replacement, but he had gone to bat for me. He said he was sure we could work something out, and he had an idea. I would have to change my performance and do exactly what he said.

I felt gutted and humiliated. Looking back on it now, it seems unlikely that the decision of whether or not to bring a play to London could have hinged on the performance of a juvenile in a minor part. But I had no previous experience of the way in which some directors manipulate performers, or why they do it. I could only think of the shame of returning to London having been fired as incompetent.

Dexter outlined his idea. He said that a short haircut, spectacles and make-up would make me as nondescript as possible. We rehearsed my new character in the afternoon and I played the part as Dexter wanted in the evening. The huge auditorium was almost empty, but a small huddle of people in the stalls seemed to be enjoying the performance. In the interval, I asked Michael Gough who they were.

'Oh, they're from Granada TV, probably *Emergency Ward Ten,*' he said, naming a popular hospital soap which was transmitted from Manchester.

My dressing-room was on the third floor. Nobody had ventured up there, except the assistant stage manager to give me the 'overture and beginners' call, so I was surprised to hear lots of feet clattering up the stone stairs after the show. I'd only just cleaned off my make-up, including the spots and freckles Dexter had suggested I should try. I was even more surprised when the people who came into my dressing-room were not known to me personally. One of them I recognised immediately as the actress, Lisa Gastoni. Mike Caine had often spoken of her; she had made a big impression on him when he'd done a day's work at Pinewood on a modest film she'd starred in. It was one of the rare times I ever heard Mike talking about anyone in hushed tones. His description of Miss Gastoni had suggested a femme fatale. He'd reported that she'd sunbathed on the lawn of the film studio, her skirt hoisted up to her thighs, her shoes abandoned on the grass. Jack-the-lad actors and extras had tried their hand at attracting her attention, but she had politely despatched them all, including Caine. 'She's one of those birds that do the pulling, there's no way anybody could lean on her,' Mike had said.

While the rest of the *Emergency Ward Ten* cast were shaking my hand and saying complimentary things about the play, Lisa hovered in the half-shadow of my dressing-room doorway. I was struck by her blonde hair and pale eyes that had enticed so many men. When the other actors started to leave, she came forward into the light. She spoke in a husky voice with only a trace of an Italian accent.

'Would you join us for a drink? We're going to the New Theatre Inn. It's just behind the theatre.' She placed her hand on my sleeve.

'Thanks. I know where it is. I'm staying there.'

'See you soon, then.'

The door closed behind her. I wished that my haircut was not so terrible; it had been chived off only hours before by a local Sweeney Todd and I wasn't used to it yet. Still, her smile was irresistible. I pulled on my jeans and the flag-blue V-neck sweater I had bought on Baxter's advice from Marks and Sparks.

199

'The New' was packed. I made my way into the saloon bar, located Lisa Gastoni and joined her crowd. Lisa started talking to me immediately, saying how she had enjoyed the show and my part in it. Whenever anyone else tried to engage me in conversation she caught my attention. At first I thought I might be imagining it, until I realised that she was circling around me, compelling me to turn my back on the others. I felt I should pinch myself to make sure it was actually happening.

When the bell rang for closing time, Lisa asked me if I'd like to drive around a bit, to unwind. Her car was parked near by; she had driven it up from London. It was a two-tone Metropolitan, small but neat with just two seats. We got in. She hitched her skirt above her knees and put the key into the ignition, talking to the car seductively, charming it to work first time.

'Ah, thirsty are you?' she said, looking at the petrol gauge on the dashboard. 'Well, we'll get you a nice long drink, right away.'

We cruised around Manchester and eventually found an all-night filling station. Lisa stood on the forecourt to supervise, and I was able to take in her figure. Mike hadn't exaggerated. Leaving the city centre, we drove off again, on to wet cobbled streets. She started complimenting me once more, not on my performance, but on my looks. No woman had ever spoken about me like this before and I kept thinking that she must be pulling my leg.

'I bet all the girls pester you, don't they?'

'Well . . . No.'

'Bet they all want to use you? Don't be shy. You can tell me.'

I looked at her profile; she seemed perfectly serious.

'Not really,' I said. I thought, I could stand being used by you, though.

She stopped the car on a side road illuminated only by a single lamp-post. It started to drizzle. She pulled a fingerless driving glove off her right hand and leaned across the car. 'Pester you to death, I bet,' she said. She drew her thumbnail down the line of my jawbone, as though etching the shape in her mind like a sculptress. She did it again, harder, digging her nail into me.

I stood it for as long as I could and then reached over for her.

When I was a boy an open-mouthed kiss had been the ultimate of imagined erotica. The mere mention of a French kiss had conjured up the whole gamut: heavy perfume, sheer stockings and satin camiknickers. I had tried on many occasions to fulfil my fantasy, but had encountered only a run of tight-lipped rejections, and it wasn't until that night that my teenage longings were satisfied.

I don't know how long we pestered each other, screened by the steamed-up windows of the car, but when I eventually made my way back to my digs the pub was closed and bolted. I had to shin up the drainpipe to get into my room, which fortunately was on the first floor front. I paced around, knowing I should be going to bed, but something nagged at me; there was something I had to do, but I couldn't recall what. I looked in the mirror and examined a fierce bruise on my neck. I thought, So *that's* what a love bite feels like.

Then I remembered my intention to check whether I looked any different. I had been taken aback by Lisa's compliments. It had seemed as though she was speaking of someone else and for a moment I thought that perhaps I had been magically transmuted into an Errol Flynn or a Gary Cooper. The person who was reflected in the mirror was still me, but a transformation had taken place. My face looked different, as though it had been lit in a cunning way to minimise its coarser aspects; the colour of my pullover gave my eyes a shine.

Perhaps it was an illusion produced by the effect of the single standard lamp on the far side of the room. After one last glance at the fetching stranger in the mirror, I climbed into bed, stretched out across the cool, unfamiliar linen and fell asleep comforted by a warm glow I hadn't known since I was little.

What a week it was! It ended on the Sunday when Lisa drove me to Leeds, our next venue. The farewell was affectionate but final. She and her Metropolitan vanished almost as rapidly as the car's four-star exhaust fumes in the chilly air. Alone again, I looked around me and studied the photos already in place outside the theatre. Leeds looked grim on that Sunday. Mike had said it had the best audience in the provinces. I hoped he was right; I needed something to lift my depression.

It was a good fifteen years before I ran into the lovely Lisa again. I had been invited to join Ibrahim Moussa – an Egyptian agent based in Rome – at one of the world's better restaurants, El

Toula. I had strolled the few hundred yards from my hotel through the soft Roman evening to Via Lupa, assuming that Moussa and I would be dining alone. He was habitually a little late, so I was surprised to find him already seated. He was accompanied by an elegant lady, and I was even more taken aback when she was introduced to me: Lisa Gastoni, a new client.

'She insisted on coming along when she found out who I was dining with,' said Ibrahim, flashing that dazzling smile which wreaked so much havoc among starlets seeking discovery in the Eternal City.

'How do you do, Miss Gastoni?' I said, trying to smile. (William Wyler once advised me that, when meeting an old flame, one must always greet her fondly, no matter how much time has passed. 'It's only polite,' said Wyler.) But it soon became clear that she did not even remotely recall meeting me, let alone that she already had my name in her book.

Michael Gough, a prince among men, drove me back to London when our tour ended in Leeds. It was one a.m. when I was dropped off at the top of the mews. Caine was up and awake. He had stayed at home to catch his favourite programme, John Freeman's *Face to Face*, on our new TV set. Thinking that I might be coming home, he had brewed a pot of tea and passed the hours watching a late showing of *The Hound of the Baskervilles* starring Basil Rathbone. God knows how much tea he'd put into the pot, but even after adding a kettleful of boiling water it still cut like iron filings.

I told him about nearly getting the chop after Edinburgh, how it had drained my confidence and made me feel sick. He just nodded sagely. Two unravelled toilet rolls in soft focus danced on to the TV screen and magically encased themselves in decorated paper. A baritone voice-over crooned, 'Doubly wrapped . . . '

Without looking around, Caine said, 'To seal the flavour in.' Flicking his eyes sideways like Bob Hope, he continued, 'It happens to everyone. Par for the course . . . Could have been worse . . . Don't think about it . . . What else?'

I told him of my brief but memorable encounter with Miss Gastoni, including being given the elbow in Leeds.

'Wow, you've really been in the wars, me old Tel,' he said, less than sympathetically. 'But that's fantastic. I know guys who'd give all their ration coupons for an hour with her – me included.' He looked me over, sizing me up.

I had been wondering whether to renew contact with the delectable lady with the pale eyes, and I sought Caine's advice on the matter.

'No, son, leave it alone. She calls the shots. She'll let you know if she's in the mood. I wouldn't hold your breath, though.' He put his arm around my shoulder. 'Nice one, Fearless . . . Here,' he said cheerfully, 'have a listen to this.' He clicked on the gramophone and dropped a new 45 on to the turntable: Johnny Tilliston's 'Poetry in Motion'.

The West End version of *This Year, Next Year* opened at the Vaudeville in the Strand. Alas, Pamela's pessimistic premonition proved accurate. The production was not well liked and I had hardly fixed my first-night telegrams to the dressing-room mirror when it was time to vacate the premises.

During the short run, however, I was invited to a party by a wealthy Swede who liked to move in showbiz circles. No one knew much about him; it was said that he liked to gamble and that he even played table-tennis for money. At this particular party in his Park Lane penthouse, I ran once more into John McGrath, the lean playwright I'd met at David Andrews's place. It was a clear night. I had taken my drink out on to the balcony and was looking across the road into the inky stillness of Hyde Park. McGrath joined me and started to describe a play he had written about the new towns and the violence spawned in the young by such featureless environments. He said he rather saw me in the lead. The play was called *Why the Chicken* and it would be directed by Lionel Bart, with music by the jazz drummer, Tony Crombie.

John offered to fix a meeting for me with the Cockney composer of *Fings Ain't Wot They Used To Be* and *Oliver*. He was as good as his word and arranged for me to meet Lionel Bart at his flat in Reece Mews. The cobbled street was between Clareville Grove and South Kensington Station. I believe the painter Francis Bacon lived next door. Lionel looked down from a first-floor window when I rang the bell and seconds later I was admitted by a blond guy with slicked-back hair who showed me up a steep flight of stairs on to which the front door opened. Bart's living-room was large and luxurious, with comprehensively carpeted floors and walls ablaze with celebrity photos and posters from Bart's hit musicals. A Cockney maid fetched cups of tea and cakes from the kitchen, on her way replenishing a cigarette box from a stack of packets on a Welsh dresser against the wall.

Lionel whizzed in accompanied by a cloud of Heure Bleu. He wore a dapper three-piece black suit, a tightly buttoned waistcoat, a shirt the colour of egg yolk and a slim black tie. His nicotine-stained fingers co-ordinated well with his shirt.

'Hi,' he said. 'I'm Li.'

'Hello Li,' I said from the deep sofa.

We shook hands. His were dry and brown.

'Wanna cigarette?' He flipped open the box.

'Sure,' I said, and I fired one up, although smoking filters wasn't really me.

Bart wanted to know about my background.

'I was born in Bow, but we moved during the War after being bombed out three times.'

'Didn't want to tempt fate, eh?' said Bart.

'That's about it. Went to Plaistow, further east.' I changed the subject. 'I used to see you playing in the Two I's. You looked different then,' I said.

'Yeah,' Bart replied, expelling smoke from his nostrils like a dragon. 'Had me hooter done.' He rubbed his renovated nose, turning sideways to display the new profile. 'Georgia Brown doesn't approve; she says I'm trying to look like a goy.'

I said, 'Some of my best chums are goys.'

Bart laughed. 'What d'you think of the piece?' he asked, lifting the tea-cosy off the pot.

'I haven't read it yet.'

'There's a couple of numbers. It's not a proper musical and I didn't write the songs. Can you sing?'

I said, 'Sure.'

He raised a sceptical black eyebrow. I liked Lionel.

He smiled without showing his teeth, reached over towards the piano and picked up a black hat, like a trilby but not as deep, and put it on, tilting it forward slightly. He lit a new cigarette from the butt of the old one.

'How well can you sing?' he wanted to know.

'Not as well as Mario Lanza, but better than Adam Faith.'

Within a week I was rehearsing *Why the Chicken* in a hall near Euston. One day I received a message to call Jimmy Fraser.

'I want you to go to the ABC in Golden Square at five-thirty today to meet Robert Lennard and Peter Ustinov. They're casting *Billy Budd*. Ustinov is going to direct it.'

'What's the part?' I wanted to know.

'The lead: Billy Budd.'

'You must be joking!'

'What?' Jimmy sounded taken aback.

'Well, he's a sort of an angel, ain't he? They must be really scraping the barrel if they want to see me.'

'They are,' said Fraser. 'They've already seen every young actor in town.'

Seventeen

Room at the Top

When I reported to the uniformed concierge at the ABC headquarters in Golden Square I was told that Mr Robert Lennard was holding his casting sessions for *Billy Budd* at a building in Lower James Street. The concierge pointed me diagonally across the gardens in the middle of the square. On my way I felt surprisingly unalarmed. I was filled with a nonchalance which stemmed from the knowledge that I had about as much chance of landing this part as I had of reaching Mecca.

Outside the building I looked up and saw a colossus staring out of a window from the third floor. It was the great Peter Ustinov. He didn't notice me. He was looking straight ahead across the slate roofs and chimney tops of Soho. I had recently read a biography of his early career. My assurance drained away and I felt small, knowing I would soon have to face such an accomplished man.

I was directed to a room on the first floor where my tentative knock was answered by a dark-haired woman.

'You must be Mr Stamp. I'm Judith Jourd, Bob Lennard's assistant. I'll take you up.'

We set off up the four flights. The stiletto heels tapped ahead of me; Mr Lennard obviously approved of a good ankle. I was shown into a room which contained a desk and three chairs. Mr Ustinov's presence made the room seem small. He turned from the window and extended a substantial hand in welcome before introducing me to Bob Lennard. Miss Jourd closed the door behind her. I sat down, lost for words. I didn't go to pieces, I was all there, but the atmosphere felt so dense that anything I said sounded weightless. After a while I just shut up. I could see Ustinov smiling at me encouragingly, but the more affable he became the further I sank into rigor mortis.

Finally, Bob Lennard looked at his watch and nodded to Peter, who looked me in the eye and said, 'We are shooting film tests at Elstree tomorrow. Would you like to do one for us?'

I nodded.

Ustinov gave an owl-like blink and grinned. He looked just like Nero in *Quo Vadis*. 'We'll get you picked up.' He looked to Bob.

'Eight o'clock,' said Bob. 'Ready for nine-thirty.' He lifted a few pages of script from the desk and handed them to me. 'If you could learn this . . . it's a scene from the film.'

I glanced at the top page. It was a dialogue between someone called Claggart and someone called Billy.

I had a touch of the vapours on the bus home. I kept trying to read the scene, but my mind was all over the place.

Caine was more excited than I was. I kept insisting that I didn't have a hope.

'Don't be a berk all your life,' snapped Caine. 'You've seen the man. You went looking dead scruffy, did a dumb interview and you've walked away with a screen test. Pipe down. Learn the words and then we'll walk it through.'

He coached me on the dialogue for two solid hours, finding key words in Claggart's speeches which would mentally trigger off my lines. When he was satisfied that I knew the scene backwards, he set about instructing me on the art of finding my mark.

'Take yer shoes off,' he said.

I did exactly as he commanded; he wasn't in any mood for argument.

'I'll put this pencil on the floor right here,' he continued. 'See where it is, and then, without looking at it, walk up to it and stop with yer toes just touching it.'

Mike's hooded eyes missed nothing. I tried several times, but on each occasion I stopped short of the mark. The third time I was still off-target.

'Why am I doing this?' I asked testily.

'We'll use something bigger.' He disappeared into the kitchen and returned with the bread-knife. 'This will give you incentive not to tread on it.'

'Why are we doing this, Mike?' I persisted.

'These marks that you keep missing are the cameraman's only way of keeping an actor in perfect focus. It is critical for the actor to hit the mark laid down. If you can't master it, you might as well give up right away. At the end of the day, if the cameraman is not satisfied with the focus you'll have to do it again. It doesn't matter how terrific you've played the take. That goes for everyone all the way up to Brando! Got it?' He almost spat the words at me. 'Everybody's had to master it somewhere along the line . . . Let's try it again.'

I was reduced to lining my toes up with the knife and pacing backwards, making a note of how many steps it took to my start mark. I had more or less mastered it before I went to bed. I couldn't do it as well as Mike, though. He could feel a chalk mark through the crêpe soles of his desert boots.

I had an old pullover that had belonged to my dad. It was a proper seaman's sweater, navy blue, which he'd kept when he left the Merchant Navy. For years he had worn it to work on the river, during which time it had endured Mum's laundering, to say nothing of the hours it had spent pegged on the washing-line stretched to twice its original size. Dad had finally given up and I inherited it. It stands out because I can't remember my dad ever giving me much in the way of presents. His name was always on my birthday and Christmas gifts, but I knew that Mum actually chose them. In fact, the only other things which Dad gave me personally were his black Crombie, which fitted me when I was fifteen, and his gold wedding ring with the diamond chip, which I received when I was twenty-one.

Anyway, I loved the old navy-blue sweater and often wore it indoors during the winter months. I don't know why I decided to wear it for the *Billy Budd* screen test, but that morning when I was scouring the fitted cupboard in our bedroom it just came to hand. Without thinking, I slipped it on over my shirt and nipped down the stairs to the car which the studio had sent for me.

I was deeply excited on that drive to Elstree and I remember being surprised that the studios were so far out of town.

When we arrived I was guided to a dressing-room and told to change into my costume by a guy who couldn't have been any older than me. There was to be no make-up. I took off my shirt and wore the sweater alone. I examined myself in the illuminated mirror. With the sweater's gaping neck and the hole under the ribs, I figured I looked as though I could have crawled up from below decks. I waited. Another young man knocked on the door and introduced himself as Claude.

'If you'll follow me, Sir, I'll take you to the set. Mr Ustinov is waiting.'

Sir. That was a good start. Claude led me along a low-ceilinged corridor to a door with a red light shining above it. Beside the light was stencilled the number '2'. He stopped. I stopped. He looked up at the light; so did I. We looked at each other. He sensed, perhaps, that I had no idea about what was going on. He cocked his head towards the light.

'They're turning over. Nobody's allowed to go in while the red light is on.'

'Turning over?'

'Shooting.'

A bell rang, and the red light went out. Claude opened the door and held it for me. I walked in, and stopped, overwhelmed by the immensity of the studio. Thirty feet above us galleries of unlit lamps hung like bats across a stage the size of a football pitch. As my eyes adjusted to the gloom, I saw that the walls were covered with padding which was held in place by diamond-shaped wire. Cables snaked across the floor.

As I followed Claude across the stage, I heard voices and laughter. Someone was saying goodbye. A figure appeared in the spill of light in one corner, then paused, found its bearings and strode towards the door with the red light above it. We passed warily, like slow-moving trains. I could hear my heart beating. Ustinov's voice grew clear as I was ushered to the enclosed square of light. Everything slowed down, the way dreams sometimes do.

The test itself was dreamlike. I realised this when I tried to recall every detail for Jimmy Fraser later. I had difficulty finding the words. We were sitting in his office; it was six-thirty and most of his staff had called it a day. 'How do you feel it went?' Jimmy asked.

I could only bring to mind the improvisation which Ustinov had sprung on me after I'd completed the test scene in which he'd played Claggart off-camera.

As soon as the camera had stopped rolling, Ustinov came on to the set and drew me conspiratorially into a corner. In a soft voice he explained that he wanted to shoot a little extra. He would insult and provoke me from behind the camera; he would accuse me of things I hadn't done, crimes I hadn't committed. I, being innocent, would be confused and bewildered by this. Because of a speech impediment, triggered by behaviour I couldn't comprehend, I would be rendered dumb. I was not to speak. Whatever happened, I must not say anything until he said, 'Cut.' He'd patted me on the shoulder and led me back to a new chalk mark that had been drawn on the floor in front of the camera.

'Stay near that,' he had said, and then, 'Whenever you're ready.'

I nodded OK. Somebody said, 'Turn over.' I heard a click and the camera started rolling. I looked at Ustinov.

'Action.'

He'd immediately started to harangue me, adopting the tone and manner of the vicious Master at Arms, Claggart. I felt as if I was being pelted with gravel. Emotions welled up inside me. I remembered the time I'd been caned at school: I had tried defiantly to say 'Thank you' but no words came out when I opened my mouth. I relived that moment briefly while listening to Claggart's torments. I found that my emotions had nowhere to go; I couldn't speak. I needed to cry out, to find some release, but, try as I might, not a sound came.

Ustinov kept pushing. Eventually the film ran out and the camera rattled to a halt. Somebody said, 'Cut.' Everyone giggled. Then it was quiet.

Ustinov had come forward and rubbed my face. 'Thank you,' he'd said. 'That was,' he'd paused, then smiled, 'tumultuous.'

'Was that all?' asked Jimmy Fraser when I had told my tale.

'That's about it.'

'Sounds good to me. I think I'll ring Judith and see what's what.'

'Will she know anything?'

'She'll know if Bob knows. He consults her on everything. She's a powerful lady.'

I went home to tell Mike. I'd only just arrived when Doug Sheldon's Sprite squealed to a halt outside. He came bounding up the stairs and I went through everything again with Mike and Doug all ears.

'How did you make out with the marks?' Mike wanted to know.

'Well, I only had to hit one. There was the chalk mark I started on and a small piece of wood they tacked to the floor about eighteen inches nearer the camera . . .'

'That was for the close-up.' Mike nodded knowingly to Doug.

' . . . which I moved on to during a line near the end.'

'Did you make it all right?' Mike enquired.

'Think so. I measured it out, and I guess I just moved on to it. I didn't think about it, really.'

'Just as it should be. Did the cameraman say anything?'

'I heard Ustinov ask him whether everything was good for him. The focus-puller nodded and he replied, "Acceptable." '

Mike was taking it all in.

'After the improvisation, I wasn't all there. I didn't notice anything! When I was getting ready to leave, an actor called Peter McEnery came into my dressing-room and asked if he could borrow my jersey.'

'That was a bit of a cheek,' said Doug.

'What did you say?' asked Mike.

'I said, "No." I wasn't feeling exactly *noblesse oblige*.'

'Well, you can't blame him for trying,' said Mike.

'Let's see the jersey,' said Doug.

I pulled it out of my holdall.

Doug put it on and looked at himself in the ornate mirror on the wall between the windows. 'You actually wore this for the test?' It didn't exactly suit him. 'He's got front, I'll say that,' he said to Mike.

'Sometimes,' Mike replied, and looked at Doug's wristwatch. 'Listen, lads. I don't want to be pushing you out, but I've got a sort coming round at eight. I don't want her to think it's a threes up.'

'Sort?' I said. 'What kind of sort? Brunette?'

'No, blonde actually. Sabra. El Al air hostess. Sergeant in the Israeli Army for a bit.'

'Didn't know you liked prickly pears,' Doug said.

'Sure you don't need back-up?' I added.

Mike wagged a forefinger at me. 'You're getting extremely lairy, my old Tel,' he grinned, 'on the strength of one film

214

test.' He turned to Doug. 'I think you'd better drive him around and cool him off a bit.'

Doug and I tumbled down the stairs, whooping and yelling like kids let off church. We had just started the car when the comely Israeli ex-sergeant strolled into the top of the mews. She was a real piece with wide shoulders and waist-length hair.

Doug said, 'She don't look like a front-wheel skid to me.'

I ruffled his Hardy Kruger hairdo. 'Neither do you, son.'

Mrs Bobroski's son let out the clutch, and we rolled off down the mews, with one last lecherous butcher's at the blonde who was ringing the bell on our pink front door.

'He's a great puller, ain't he, ole Mike?' I said.

'Dynamite,' agreed Doug, sliding the aviator shades from his James Dean windbreaker pocket, and putting them on, even though by now it was quite dark.

Doug had always understood my preference for aimless cruising with no particular place to go. In my case, I suppose I was trying to relive those times with my old mate Lee in his Lea-Francis, but it slotted in nicely with Doug's own preoccupation for just tooling around. He was one of those people who are born to drive. It didn't matter much to him where or what his living quarters were as long as his sports car was ticking over outside with a tiger in its tank.

This evening, however, he had planned an excursion. Under a bridge on the Embankment, where we stopped to put the top on when it started to rain, he informed me that he was treating me to a bath, or *vunni* as he termed it. I was about to become familiar with what was, in my opinion, the greatest Turkish bath ever built.

Doug parked the car in Bloomsbury Place. I followed him across Southampton Row into the old Imperial Hotel. Down the stairs of that noble old hostelry a passageway led to the bottle-green chamber housed in the basement. The tiles alone would have been worth the visit. We undressed and made for the hottest steam room. I wrapped myself in the traditional blue chequered loin-cloth and Doug swathed himself in several royal cubits of cotton towelling. He couldn't take as much heat as me, and pulled part of the towel over his head like a cowl.

I flopped down on the smooth, worn marble bench that bordered three sides of the hot room and slumped against the rich tiles, letting my body absorb the clouds of vapour. My system relaxed. The stored tension started to be released. I felt as though I was slipping into a trance. I peered across the room at Doug. Through the clouds of steam he resembled a monk in contemplation. His face was flushed and perspiring. I smiled, but his attention was elsewhere, as though he was listening to a neighbour's music.

Not quite looking at me, he said, 'I think you're gonna get this . . . '

'This what?'

'This part. Billy whatever he's called; you're gonna get it. It's come for you.'

The knowledge appeared to sadden him.

'Cheer up, me old china,' I said. 'Come the revolution, there'll be room at the top for all of us.'